RHODE ISLAND
Real Estate Basics

Dearborn™

Real Estate Education

While a great deal of care has been taken to provide accurate and current information, the ideas, suggestions, general principles, and conclusions presented in this text are subject to local, state, and federal laws and regulations, court cases, and any revisions of same. The reader is urged to consult legal counsel regarding any points of law. This publication should not be used as a substitute for competent legal advice.

Senior Vice President and General Manager: Roy Lipner
Publisher and Director of Distance Learning: Evan M. Butterfield
Editorial Project Consultant: Marie Spodek, DREI
Development Editor: Amanda Rahn
Editorial Production Manager: Bryan Samolinski
Creative Director: Lucy Jenkins
Cover and Text Design: Gail Chandler

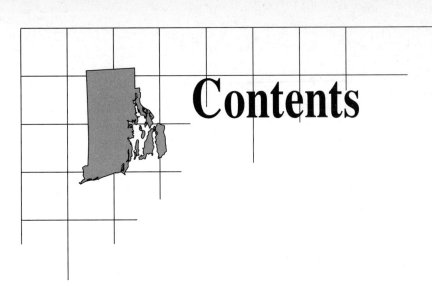

Contents

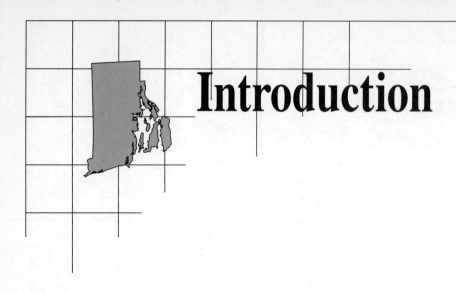

Introduction

Over the last century, all 50 states and the District of Columbia have enacted laws, rules, and regulations to govern the real estate profession. These laws have been enacted to protect the public—buyers, sellers, landlords, and tenants—from dishonest, careless, or unethical practices by real estate licensees. Essentially, the laws provide a framework to ensure that licensees are competent and engage in acceptable business behaviors. Across the United States, some of these laws and regulations are so similar that they can be considered "national" or "generic" real estate principles. Many of the important details, however, vary greatly among the states. In order to ensure both professional competency and that you pass the licensing exam, it's vital that you understand both the "big picture" principles *and* the state-specific details.

This book has been primarily designed to supplement a general real estate principles text, and on page vi you will find a convenient correlation table that illustrates where the general topics are addressed in a variety of other publications. However, *Rhode Island Real Estate Basics* also provides a valuable overview of state law and practice when used on its own.

No book writes itself. Like a real estate transaction, this book is the product of teamwork and cooperation among professionals. The following individuals contributed their expertise, industry knowledge, and practical insight to this book.

About the Author

Monica S. Staaf, Esq., is an attorney who is currently practicing in Rhode Island. She is a member of the Massachusetts, New Hampshire, and Rhode Island bars. She is the Legal Counsel/Lobbyist for the Rhode Island Association of REALTORS®. Monica previously served as General Counsel for the Massachusetts Association of REALTORS® and Associate Counsel for the Home Builders Association of Massachusetts in addition to representing real estate licensees in private legal practice. She is also a real estate educator and has given numerous seminars to REALTORS® on topics such as lead paint, agency, fair housing, and contract law.

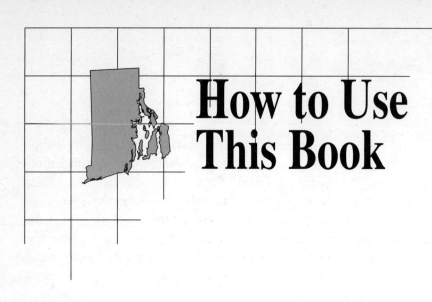

How to Use This Book

The conversion table below provides a quick and easy reference for *Rhode Island Real Estate Basics* in conjunction with various principles books. For instance, *Rhode Island Real Estate Basics'* Chapter 2, "Operating a Real Estate Business," may be read in conjunction with Chapter 5 in *Modern Real Estate Practice;* Chapter 7 in *Real Estate Fundamentals;* Chapter 13 in *Mastering Real Estate Principles;* and Lesson 13 in *SuccessMaster™* software.

Rhode Island Real Estate Basics	*Modern Real Estate Practice,* 15th Edition	*Real Estate Fundamentals,* 5th Edition	*Mastering Real Estate Principles,* 3rd Edition	*SuccessMaster™* (National) Software
1. Licensing Overview	—	—	16	16
2. Operating a Real Estate Business	5, 20	7, 9, 15	13, 14, 16, 17	13, 14, 17
3. Agency Overview	4, 5, 6, 17	9	13, 24	13, 24
4. Contracts And Closings Overview	6, 10, 11, 13, 21, 22	6, 7, 10, 16, 17	3, 10, 11, 12, 14	3, 10, 11, 12, 14
5. License Law Enforcement Overview	4, 5	—	13, 16	13, 16
6. Specialty Topics	8, 16, 18	5, 8, 11	8, 9, 18	8, 9, 18
7. Title Issues	7, 10, 19	3, 10, 14	3, 4, 5	3, 4, 5, 26

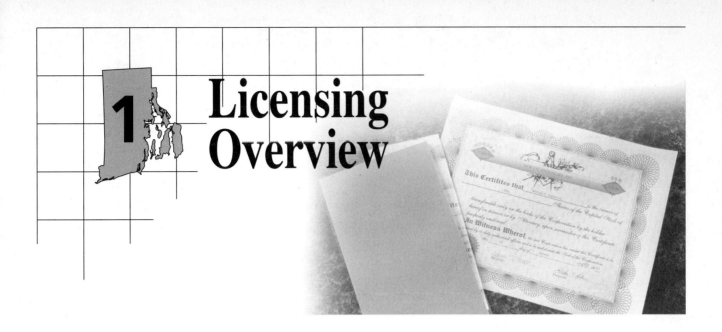

1 Licensing Overview

The statutory law that governs real estate practices in Rhode Island is Rhode Island General Law 5-20.5 (www.rilin.state.ri.us/Statutes/Statutes.html). This law gives the Rhode Island Department of Business Regulation the authority to adopt reasonable rules and regulations to carry out its purposes."

The rules and regulations found at www.dbr.state.ri.us/real_estate have the same force and effect as the law and provide more detail for the administration of the law and guidelines for the real estate licensee. The Rhode Island Commercial Licensing Regulation 11 governs the real estate practices of real estate brokers and salespersons. Commercial Licensing Regulation 10 covers the activities of appraisers.

This first chapter covers the licensing agency and licensing issues: activities requiring licensure and exemptions, license categories, and licensing requirements and renewals.

A. Rhode Island Real Estate Commission

1.A.1 What is the name of the Rhode Island real estate regulatory body?

The Real Estate Division of the Department of Business Regulation (DBR) licenses and regulates real estate licensees. The Real Estate Commission acts as an advisory board to the DBR.

The DBR's web site address is located at www.dbr.state.ri.us. One may write or fax the DBR at The Department of Business Regulation, 233 Richmond

Street, Providence, Rhode Island 02902. Phone: (401) 222-2246; Fax: (401) 222-6098.

1.A.2 How many members are on the commission? How long may they serve?

The Rhode Island Real Estate Commission is composed of nine commissioners who serve five-year terms. The governor of Rhode Island appoints seven of the nine commissioners. The two remaining commissioners are ex-officio members of the commission who have full voting rights: (1) the attorney general or his/her designee; and (2) the director of DBR or his/her designee.

By statute, members cannot be appointed to succeed themselves for more than one term, i.e., no one may serve more than ten years. A commissioner appointed to fill a vacancy finishes the remaining term of the departing commissioner.

Specifically, commission members must come from different counties. Three of the commissioners must have worked as a real estate broker in Rhode Island for at least ten years prior to his/her appointment to the commission. Four of the commissioners must be members of the general public. To further vary the make up of the commission, at least one of the four must have "substantial academic experience" in real estate and at least one must have been active in a citizen's group, such as a consumer advocacy group, that addresses real estate issues.

By law, commissioners are to be paid $25 per day a long with out-of-pocket expenses incurred in performing his or her duties as a commissioner. However, due to state budgetary issues, members typically do not receive this stipend.

1.A.3 Who does the day-to-day work?

Like most organizations, there are others who help facilitate internal operations. The Associate Director of the Commercial Licensing and Regulation Division of DBR is empowered to hire and provide staff to assist the commission with implementing the law. The Administrator of the Real Estate Division and his/her small staff handle the day-to-day operations and report to the Associate Director, Commercial Licensing and Regulations Division of DBR.

The director of DBR or his/her designee is by statute an ex-officio member of the commission with full voting rights. The current Real Estate Administrator is an ex-officio member of the commission as the designee of the director of DBR. Key staff may be identified on the home page: www.dbr.state.ri.us.

1.A.4 The DBR real estate section is charged with what statutory duties?

According to the home page, the Division of Commercial Licensing and Regulation is "responsible for the licensing and regulation of Real Estate salespersons, brokers, and appraisers. To this end, the division coordinates and administers examinations for real estate brokers, salesperson, and real estate appraisers. Additionally, the section is responsible for issuing licenses/certificates/permits to real estate branch offices, real estate schools, and out-of-state land sales. The section is also empowered to investigate and adjudicate complaints to insure license compliance with Rhode Island State laws, rules, and regulations."

The real estate commission can recommend regulatory changes to DBR, recommend approval of continuing education courses, review proposed real estate test questions, all subject to DBR approval. However, DBR has no obligation to defer to the wishes of the commission; such decisions are all subject to DBR approval. The DBR holds disciplinary hearings and promulgates rules and regulations.

The Rhode Island General Law can only be changed by a vote of the legislature, called the general assembly, and signed by the governor. On the other hand, the commission may recommend to the DBR changes to the rules and regulations from time to time, which can be amended by DBR without approval from the general assembly.

B.   Licensing Issues

1.B.1 In Rhode Island, who is required to hold a real estate license?

In Rhode Island, anyone who engages in the following activities with the expectation of being paid and does not qualify for an exemption must hold either a broker or salespersons real estate license:

- Directs or assists with the procuring of prospects for a real estate transaction
- Lists, sells, rents, auctions real estate
- Appraises residential real estate containing four or fewer units
- Holds himself or herself out to be involved in these activities

Also, a person who is employed by the owners of lots or other parcels of land must be licensed.

1.B.2   What is the largest exception to the licensing requirements?

The most important exemption is the person who acts on his or her own behalf. Any person can list, buy, rent, or sell his or her own property. The state does not regulate such a transaction, reasoning that if the owner makes a mistake, the owner may only blame himself or herself, no one else.

Also, by extension, **anyone who is employed by the owner of the property on a regular basis** is exempt from having to be licensed to perform acts that are in the regular course of his or her regular employment or incidental to it. Examples include buying, selling, or managing property owned, rented, leased, or to be acquired or sold by this owner.

1.B.3   Are there any other exemptions to the licensing requirements?

Yes, Rhode Island license law specifically exempts the following as well:

- Attorney in fact acting under the authorized authority of a **power of attorney** to act on behalf of the owner or purchaser of a property
- Attorneys admitted to practicing law in Rhode Island only when advising the party to a real estate transaction as an incident to the practice of law
- Receiver, trustee in bankruptcy, administrator or executor, or any other person under court jurisdiction
- Guardians and other fiduciaries

Please note that attorneys who engage in the acts of a broker must comply with licensing requirements. This is as opposed to limiting themselves to giving legal advice as noted in the above exemption. However, the attorneys who is licensed as an attorney in Rhode Island is not required to pass the broker's examination.

The exemptions make no specific reference to time-share property. However, generally, selling time-shares falls under the category of employees working for owners of property.

1.B.4   Does Rhode Island recognize licensure in other states?

Reciprocity agreements exist between states that have similar licensing requirements to those in Rhode Island and where similar recognition and courtesies are extended to each other. Rhode Island recognizes licenses from other states to a limited extent.

If an applicant has held a real estate broker or salesperson's license for a minimum of two years from a state that grants reciprocity to Rhode Island licensees, the licensee is exempt from taking the "uniform" portion of the

Rhode Island broker or salesperson's examination. However, the licensee must still pass the state-specific, Rhode Island portion of the examination.

There is a special section for nonresident or out-of-state licensees. A nonresident broker need not have an office in Rhode Island as long as he or she has one that is open to the public in another state. A nonresident must file a power of attorney with the Department of Business Regulation for purposes of accepting service of process. Simply stated, if a legal action is initiated, the licensee cannot request a change of venue.

If the home-state license of a nonresident Rhode Island licensee is revoked or suspended, the licensee must notify the Rhode Island Real Estate commission. A hearing may be held to determine whether similar disciplinary action should be taken against the nonresident Rhode Island licensee.

1.B.5 How does a corporation or partnership receive a real estate license?

A broker's license that is issued to a corporation, partnership, association, trust, or limited liability corporation must designate the name of a principal broker, who is a principal, active officer of the entity. All other brokers and salespeople who are associated with the entity must hold their own licenses.

1.B.6 What is the difference between a salesperson and a broker? Can there be more than one broker in any given office?

The practices of the real estate industry are similar to the old master craftsman/apprentice system of years ago. Real estate licensees start out with a salesperson's license working under the direct supervision of a broker. Rhode Island law requires that a person hold an active salesperson's license for at least one year before becoming eligible to receive a broker's license. However, this requirement is waived if the applicant has:

- a baccalaureate (BS, BA, etc.) in real estate from an accredited college or university, or
- completed a minimum of 90 hours from a DBR-approved school.

There is only one designated broker in any office. When the license law refers to a broker, it is referring to this individual. The other licensees ("associates") in the office may hold a salesperson's or broker's (aka "broker associate") licenses. The broker may be the owner or a manager. The broker is responsible for the escrow fund trust account and for the real estate activities conducted by the associates in this office.

The public has the right to know that there is a person in charge locally. This person will be identified as the broker-in-charge on the office license, required by law to be prominently displayed for public inspection. Even if the office is owned by another entity in another city, the local broker is responsible for the escrow funds held by that office and the activities of each person licensed in that office. All brokerage contracts are in the name of the broker even if other licensees in the office actually sign the agreement.

1.B.7 List the basic requirements for a real estate license.

In order to become a real estate salesperson or broker, the applicant must

- be a citizen or legal resident of the United States;
- be 18 years or older;
- file an application with the Department of Business Regulation;
- pay a fee of $10;
- submit recommendations of at least three citizens who have been property owners for at least three years, and who have known the applicant for three years; and
- pass a written real estate salesperson's or broker's examination.

An applicant for a broker's license must also prove that he or she has worked full time as a real estate salesperson for at least a year prior to filing a license application. As previously mentioned, this requirement may be waived if the applicant has a four-year college degree in real estate or has completed at least 90 hours of classroom study in a school permitted by the Department of Business Regulation. The DBR can also require the applicant to submit additional proof that he or she has a good reputation, is honest, and is competent.

An applicant for either license must also pay a $25 fee to the Real Estate Recovery Fund.

1.B.8 List reasons that the commission may deny a license.

The DBR may deny a license based on character issues, i.e., dishonesty, untrustworthiness, failure of the examination, failure to comply with statutory requirements, etc. If the license application is denied, the applicant and DBR must follow the same procedures that are outlined in Chapter 5, Enforcement, to contest the denial.

Fees remitted with an application for licensure are refunded if the commission finds the applicant was not qualified for a license.

1.B.9 Will the commission make any exceptions if the applicant has a blemish on his or her record?

Possibly, yes. If denied a license, the applicant has 30 days to request a discovery hearing. The Rhode Island Real Estate Commission will consider the nature of an offense, any documented aggravating or extenuating circumstances, time lapsed, rehabilitation, treatment, and restitution performed before denying or revoking a liccnsc.

1.B.10   Are there any special duties imposed on brokers?

A broker who sponsors a salesperson during the salesperson's first year of licensure must be able to demonstrate that the broker has the time available and experience necessary to adequately supervise an inexperienced salesperson. The broker is responsible for ensuring that all the provided real estate related preprinted documents and forms are legal, correct, and current. The designated broker is responsible for the escrow deposit account.

1.B.11   Do the affiliated salespeople and brokers have any responsibilities?

Each actively licensed broker associate and salesperson is licensed under a designated broker. In addition, a commission rule requires that each salesperson and broker associate keep his or her broker fully informed regarding real estate related matters. A licensee who fails to do so could be subject to disciplinary action.

1.B.12   Can a salesperson or associate broker be licensed under more than one broker?

No, a broker associate or a salesperson cannot be licensed under more than one broker during the same time period. Moreover, in the situation of a licensee who hires a licensed personal assistant, both must be licensed under the same broker.

1.B.13   What are specific requirements for an applicant to obtain a salesperson's license?

As a practical matter, the vast majority of applicants for a salesperson's license do take a prelicensing class to prepare themselves for the Real Estate Licensing Examination, but they are not legally required to do so. The examination is a two-part examination: (1) Basic Modern Real Estate Practices and (2) Rhode Island Real Estate Law. Both parts are taken at one sitting, and the applicant must score 70 percent or better on both parts to receive a license. An applicant who fails one part is required to retest only on the part failed. All applicants receive only a pass or fail score. ASI does not provide percentage correct scores.

All of the requirements for these applicants are listed below (excluding the contribution to the Real Estate Recovery Fund and insurance requirements.) As an added check, the DBR Web site contains the salesperson's application form that states the requirements.

Under **§ 5-20.5-3,** applicants applying for the first time for a license to act as a real estate broker or real estate salesperson must file an application furnished by the director. The basic application for either license asks for the applicant's age, residence, place of business and present occupation, and occupation for the past five (5) years. As previously mentioned, the applicant must be a citizen or legal resident of the United States and the legal age of majority, if applicant for the broker license, or at least eighteen (18) years of age for the salesperson license.

The applicant must also indicate if and whether the applicant has been refused a real estate broker's or salesperson's license in Rhode Island or in any other state or had any real estate license suspended or revoked. The applicant must swear under oath that the information is true and accurate.

Additionally, the broker applicant must include recommendations from at least three (3) citizens who have owned property for at least three (3) years and who have known the applicant for three (3) years, and are not related to the applicant. These recommendations must certify that the applicant bears a good reputation for honesty and trustworthiness and a statement recommending that a license be granted to the applicant.

The additional requirement for a salesperson applicant is a sworn statement from a broker stating that the broker believes that the applicant is competent and trustworthy and a recommendation that the applicant be given a salesperson's license.

The processing fee is $10 for either application (broker or salesperson).

1.B.14   Name the additional requirements to become a broker.

The broker candidate must be actively licensed as a salesperson for at least 12 months. Qualified applicants for a **broker's** license must complete a commission-approved course of at least 90 classroom hours prior to taking the broker's examination. This requirement may be waived as previously mentioned.

1.B.15   Who administers the real estate exam?

The exam is prepared and administered by Assessments Systems, Inc. (ASI), P.O. Box 8588, Philadelphia, PA 19101-8588.

1.B.16   Who pays for the exam?

The candidate pays the examination fee directly to the testing service. The commission establishes with the testing service the examination fees based on administration costs.

1.B.17   May a candidate who fails the exam retake it?

A person who fails to pass the exam or either portion is allowed to immediately retake the exam (or section) by telephoning or filing a new registration form and paying the examination fee. There is no limit to the number of times that the applicant may take the exam.

1.B.18   What is the next step after the person passes the exam?

An applicant must submit a license application prior to sitting for either the broker's or salesperson's examination. The DBR will notify the applicant of his or her exam results within 30 days after taking the exam. If the applicant passes, he or she must submit the license fee to DBR within one year after the date of the exam. If this license fee is not paid within one year of completing (and passing) his or her broker's or salesperson's exam, the applicant must retake the examination.

1.B.19   How are license fees determined?

With few exceptions, i.e., branch office license, license fees are established by the Rhode Island General Assembly and not by the Department of Business Regulation. In addition to the $10 application fee, an applicant for a broker's license must pay $120 for a two-year license. The applicant for a salesperson's license must pay $80 for a two-year license.

1.B.20   Can the first-time applicant ask for an inactive license?

No, initial applicants are not allowed to file for an "inactive" license. The applicant must first receive an active license that may then be placed on inactive status. Individuals whose licenses are on inactive status with the Rhode Island Real Estate Commission are not required to carry errors and omissions insurance nor are they obligated to take continuing education courses. Of course, they may not assist in any real estate activities for which a license is required.

1.B.21   When does a real estate license expire?

All licenses are renewed on April 30th of every even-numbered year. If an applicant receives a license in an odd-numbered year, he or she must renew this license April 30th of the following even-numbered year.

1.B.22   Does the commission do a credit check?

There are no credit check or finger printing requirements for this license. However, character references are required, but they cannot be obtained from real estate licensees. Character references must come from outside the real estate profession from a person who has owned property for at least three years and who has known the candidate for at least three years.

1.B.23   Are there any residency or citizenship requirements?

In Rhode Island, applicants for a broker's license or salesperson's license must be U.S. citizens or legal residents of the United States.

1.B.24   How is a license renewed?

Renewal applications are mailed in March of every even-numbered year by first-class mail to each licensee whose license is due for renewal. However, failure to receive the renewal notice does not relieve the licensee of this duty to renew. The licensee must submit the application form and pay the appropriate renewal fee.

The fees for renewal licenses are the same for initial licenses. The broker must pay $120 for a two-year license; a salesperson must pay $80 for a two-year license. If the renewal form and fees are submitted late, a broker must pay a $15 reinstatement fee and a salesperson must pay a $10 reinstatement fee. Applicants must submit proof of completion of continuing education classes and proof of errors and omissions insurance.

1.B.25   How many continuing education hours are required for active status renewal?

DBR increased the number of mandatory continuing education hours in 2002. The increase affects those in the licensing renewal cycle that started on July 1, 2002.

All licensees must take a total of 18 "clock" hours of continuing education classes. Six of the hours must be taken in core classes: Law of Agency, Law of Contracts, Fair Housing, Lead Hazard Mitigation, and Rhode Island License Law and Ethics. The remaining hours are elective and may be taken in a variety of classes that have been approved by the real estate commission. These hours cannot be carried over to another license term. The applicant must certify the hours and courses taken on the application and attach certificates from real estate schools for each class that he or she completed.

For licenses renewed after July 1, 2004, licensees will be required to demonstrate their familiarity with their duties relating to the Lead Poisoning Prevention Act and the Lead Hazard Mitigation Act. This requirement will be further explained once DBR adopts lead regulations.

1.B.26 Is there any alternative to attending continuing education classes for renewal purposes?

Licensees who obtained a license prior to December 27, 1984 are "grandfathered" from this requirement. Brokers who are attorneys and licensees who have been licensed for less than 180 days prior to the expiration of their license are also exempt. Also, the Department of Business Regulation has approved the concept of "distance learning" that allows licensees to take classes online. The distance learning classes must follow ARELLO guidelines.

1.B.27 What are the consequences if the license is not timely renewed?

If the licensee fails to renew by the appropriate April 30th expiration date, then the license expires. The person is given a grace period to renew by paying a $15 or $10 reinstatement fee in addition to the regular renewal fee. However, since the license expired on April 30th, no real estate business can be conducted until a new "active" license is issued. In other words, the grace period is **to renew,** but **not to act.**

C.   Licensee Duties and Responsibilities

1.C.1 Who keeps track of each license?

The DBR maintains records of all licenses. Each affiliate's license must be displayed in the broker's office. Each licensee is responsible for maintaining active licensure and for fulfilling renewal duties.

1.C.2 Is it legal for a licensee to buy and/or sell property for his or her own portfolio?

Rhode Island law prohibits licensees from acting in a dual capacity of both an agent and an **undisclosed** principal in any transaction. Without disclosure, there is a conflict of interest and an appearance of impropriety. A licensee must disclose that he or she intends to purchase directly or indirectly, i.e., through a third party "straw" buyer any property that is listed with his or her firm. However, the statute and regulations are silent with respect to sale of real estate or purchase of property outside the firm.

Rule 20 requires a licensee to reveal *conflicts of interest* in writing. Rhode Island law requires that the created conflict of interest be discussed with both the seller-client and the buyer-client at the time of or prior to the licensee's solicitation of confidential information or prior to an offer being made by the buyer or prior to an acceptance by the seller. Thus, licensees are allowed to purchase property from seller-clients or sell property owned by them to buyer-clients **only if** the licensee includes a clearly written disclosure describing the licensee's true position to the other party.

Other than adhering to the REALTOR® Code of Ethics, there is no specific legal requirement for a licensee to disclose that he or his family members own or wish to purchase property. Rule 20 (above) indirectly touches upon this issue by requiring a licensee to disclose conflicts of interest in writing. Also, agency law requires licensees to treat consumers fair and honestly. If the licensee has any doubts, it is best to disclose.

1.C.3 May licensees sell or buy property for themselves without going through their brokers?

This matter is addressed by office policy. In Rhode Island, without broker participation, licensed agents are allowed by commission rule to sell their own property. If no brokerage fees are to be paid and it is strictly a "for sale by owner" transaction, and the licensee does not function as a licensee in any capacity throughout the transaction, then a licensee could advertise his or her property without including the name of his or her broker.

Should a licensee choose to sell their real property as a for sale by owner (FSBO), then any involved deposit money could be written directly to the owner/licensee. However, in this case, it would be advisable for the seller's attorney to hold the deposit until the transaction closes.

1.C.4 What happens if a licensee sells his or her own property through their broker's office?

This is also a matter of office policy. License law does not prohibit a licensee from acting as a FSBO. Many companies do have office policies requiring licensees to buy or sell their own real estate to limit any liability to the company. If listed, then the licensee negotiates the commission structure.

1.C.5   *Under what conditions may a real estate licensee hire a support person (personal assistant)?*

Many licensees hire a support person(s) to assist them. These assistants may be licensed or not licensed. The state of Rhode Island does not require companies to adopt a written policy with respect to the use of personal assistants.

1.C.6   *Who is legally responsible for the activities performed by the personal assistant?*

The principal broker is responsible for every real estate transaction in which his company or agents participates. Therefore, the principal broker is ultimately responsible for the acts of a personal assistant who may be employed by the broker or a licensee affiliated with the broker.

1.C.7   *What are some of the activities that an unlicensed person may perform?*

The proper role of an unlicensed personal assistant is that of an administrative assistant or secretary. Under the direct supervision of a licensee, Rhode Island law permits unlicensed assistants to answer the telephone, schedule appointments, and provide listing information to other licensees as well as to forward calls from the public to a licensee. An unlicensed assistant can perform bookkeeping functions.

Unlicensed assistants may also perform the following duties with licensee's direct supervision and approval:

- Write advertising copy and promotional material
- Type and copy purchase and sales agreements, listing agreements, etc.
- Submit listing data to the multiple-listing-service (MLS)
- Check on the status of closing files
- Prepare closing packages
- Have keys made
- Maintain files
- Install or remove signs on property
- Act as a courier by delivering documents to buyers and sellers
- Schedule appointments with the seller or seller's agent in order to show the property
- Arrange dates and times for inspections, mortgage applications, walk-through inspections, and closings

1.C.8   What activities are specifically prohibited for an unlicensed assistant?

Unlicensed personal assistants cannot make representations about real estate except for transmitting published information. Personal assistants may fax, e-mail, or deliver written listing information, brochures, seller disclosure forms, etc., to prospective buyers or real estate licensees from other firms but cannot answer questions about the property.

Unlicensed persons may not show rental property or real estate that is for sale. They may not "host or conduct an open house without being accompanied at all times by a licensee." For example, a personal assistant can sit at an open house to sign in prospective buyers or hand them written listing information but cannot show them around the house or point out features of the house.

The unlicensed assistant cannot prepare or present a comparable market analysis (CMA). However, a personal assistant can do research on "sold" properties, obtain tax information, etc., to assist his or her broker or salespeople preparing CMAs.

The unlicensed assistant cannot receive payment or commissions that are tied to the sale or rental of real estate. An unlicensed personal assistant should be paid a flat or hourly rate rather than a percentage of a transaction. The payment cannot be contingent on the successful closing or rental of a property. Nor can the assistant negotiate or answer questions about the terms of a sale, rental, or purchase of a property. An unlicensed assistant cannot explain the meaning of a home inspection contingency, seller disclosure form, agency disclosure form, etc., to a consumer.

One final note, just to clarify: Unlicensed personal assistants are not allowed to hold themselves out in any manner as being licensed or affiliated with a particular firm or real estate business. In other words, they are not allowed to print their names on real estate company business cards in an attempt to deceive the public.

1.C.9   Can a brokerage use a lottery to market property?

The selling of chances (lotteries) by a real estate brokerage firm is illegal in Rhode Island. The brokerage may not offer free lots, or conduct lotteries or contests for the purpose of influencing a buyer or prospective buyer of real property.

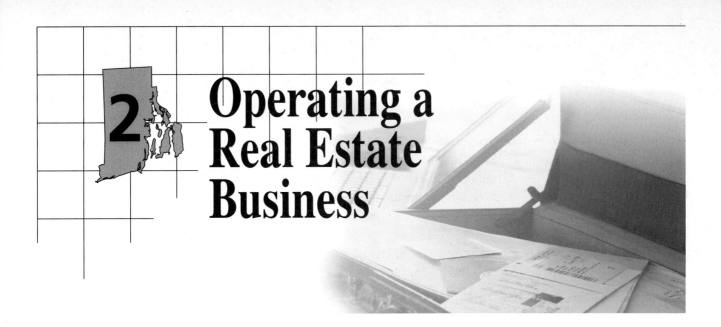

2 Operating a Real Estate Business

With a broker's license, one may open and operate a real estate business. The broker may hire those holding either a salesperson's or broker associate's license, although the principal broker is ultimately responsible for the actions of affiliated licensees. This chapter covers the additional rules and regulations for brokers regarding advertising and escrow fund trust accounts. Additionally, real estate licensees must comply with state variations to federal laws. These variations to Federal Fair Housing and Megan's Law are noted.

A. Office Licenses

2.A.1 What licenses are required before a broker can open an office?

A real estate broker must hold a valid broker's license in order to run his own business. All principal brokers (as opposed to associate brokers or salespeople) must maintain an office that is open to the public during regular business hours.

Because the office must comply with local zoning requirements, it cannot be located in the broker's house unless local zoning permits this use. If it is located in a home, it must have "direct access" to the office or a separate entrance that is visible from the street. Brokers should check with their town or city zoning office to confirm that the property complies with local zoning requirements and determine whether any local permits, such as business and sign permits, are also required.

2.A.2   How does a corporation or partnership receive a real estate license?

Corporations, partnerships, and associations may apply for a separate real estate broker's license from the Department of Business Regulation. This section of the statute does not specifically mention limited liability companies (LLCs) and limited liability partnerships (LLPs) although they are valid business models in Rhode Island and referenced in DBR regulations, i.e., in Rule 2.

The license must designate the name of a "principal active officer," i.e., president, clerk, general partner, etc., of the company for whom the license is valid. All other active participants must be licensed as a broker or salesperson.

2.A.3   How many licenses must a branch office have?

At a minimum, a branch office must have at least two licenses: a broker's license and a branch office license. There can be any number of licensees affiliated with the office, or there could be just one broker. A principal broker must apply for a license for each branch office. Each branch office must be under the direct supervision of a broker who is designated as the "office supervisor" and must comply with the zoning and other requirements stated above.

B.   Advertising Rules

2.B.1   What is a blind ad? Is it legal in Rhode Island?

In Rhode Island, a "blind ad" is one where a brokerage firm or listing agent includes just his or her own name or a post office box number or a telephone number in order to bait readers into believing that the advertised property is a private party. This unscrupulous practice is illegal.

All brokers, when advertising real estate, must use their regular business name and unmistakably indicate that the party is a real estate broker and not a private party. Real estate advertising must be honest. It should never be misleading, deceptive, or intentionally misrepresent any property, terms, values, or policies and services of the brokerage. In print advertising, a salesperson's name must appear in print that is smaller than the name of the company.

2.B.2 Are there special requirements for a real estate office or individual licensees to advertise on the Internet?

No, at the present time, there are no specific rules. However, brokers who advertise on the Internet should make sure that the advertising does not lead to charges of blind ads.

2.B.3 Under what circumstances may a brokerage place a For Sale sign?

A broker may place a For Sale sign on a property only with permission of the owner or his authorized agent. Failure to remove a sign when requested violates a DBR rule and is subject to disciplinary action in the form of a civil penalty. After a sold listing closes, the broker or salesperson must remove the sign unless the new owner permits it to remain.

C. Trust Accounts

2.C.1 What are escrow funds, and what can a broker do with them?

Escrow funds are funds that belong to someone else. In Rhode Island, these monies are commonly referred to as "escrow funds" or "deposits." Every Rhode Island-based real estate brokerage firm that expects to handle funds belonging to others must maintain an escrow account that is separate from business and personal accounts.

2.C.2 Where can escrow funds be located?

Escrow account funds must be deposited in a Rhode Island "depository institution." The depository can be a bank, savings and loan association, savings bank, or credit union.

2.C.3 How soon must escrow funds be deposited?

All funds belonging to others, except those agreed to between contracting parties, must be deposited into the broker's escrow account by no later than **five (5) banking days** after the **last signature of acceptance.** This dated instrument could be an offer to purchase, a rental agreement, a lease, an exchange, or even an option. However, prior to obtaining *the last signature,* it is customary to deposit checks in the transaction file of the listing broker.

2.C.4   How should deposit money be handled when one office has the listing, and another office is working with the buyer?

The deposit check should be made payable to the listing broker's escrow account, period. Otherwise, the cooperating agent risks liability in the event of a deposit dispute.

2.C.5   What are the rules when the buyer wants to use a postdated check or a diamond ring for a deposit?

There are no statutory rules in Rhode Island that address this issue. However, postdated checks or anything other than cash or an immediately cashable check should not be accepted as a deposit unless that fact is so communicated to the seller prior to the acceptance of the offer and is so stated in the offer to purchase.

2.C.6   What are the rules governing an escrow account?

Escrow account funds must be held separately (i.e., not commingled) with other personal and business accounts of the licensee. Whenever a licensee is in doubt as to whether funds received should be deposited into their broker's trust account, the safest course of action is to account for those funds in the broker's trust account.

2.C.7   Money in the escrow account can earn a lot of interest. Who gets the interest?

Unless there is a written agreement to the contrary, the broker may retain any interest accrued from deposits. In practice, buyers and sellers in Rhode Island rarely request or receive interest.

2.C.8   How can a broker open an escrow trust account without any escrow trust funds?

The state of Rhode Island allows brokerage firms to open escrow accounts using personal funds. A broker may maintain nominal personal or business funds in an escrow account to meet minimal balance requirements of the bank or government.

2.C.9   What is commingling of funds and why is it illegal?

By definition, *commingling* is mixing personal funds with those belonging to other people. To repeat, the broker's personal or business account is to be used solely for paying expenses directly related to the maintenance of the escrow trust account. Any amount in excess of "nominal" is considered **commingling.**

The problem with excess personal funds in the broker's escrow account is simple. If the broker commingled personal funds into this account and the Internal Revenue Service (IRS) froze the broker's accounts, then the escrow account would be frozen too. The same thing could happen if a sole proprietor owned the brokerage and the sole proprietor suddenly died after commingling personal funds into the trust account. The commingled brokerage escrow account could end up in probate.

In either event, all closings would be tied up for a considerable length of time. To avoid these potential problems, brokers may not keep more than a nominal amount in this escrow account.

2.C.10   What happens to unclaimed escrow funds?

Unclaimed funds could ultimately be transferred to the state treasurer's office, but many brokers prefer to hold the funds "just in case."

2.C.11   What may not be paid directly out of the escrow account?

It should be noted that the broker should never use the escrow account as his or her business operating account or for personal uses. Monies that may not be disbursed directly from this account would include salaries and normal business or operational expenses. The broker can pay company commissions or commissions to other companies from the escrow account.

2.C.12   What is the procedure for disbursing escrow funds?

As a general rule, no funds can be disbursed from the escrow account prior to the closing without the written consent of all the parties. In the event of a dispute over the return of forfeiture of any earnest money or escrow deposit held by the broker, the broker is required to hold the deposit in the escrow account until he receives written consent from both parties.

2.C.13   What is an example of money in and out of an escrow account?

It is possible for a broker to place a deposit into the escrow account and at closing, with written permission, transfer the deposit to the brokerage account in lieu of commission earned. For example, a broker listed a house for a $12,000 commission. It sold for full price, and a $12,000 deposit check was written and deposited into the broker's escrow account.

DBR regulations allow the listing broker to apply the $12,000 deposit that is located in the escrow account towards the commission that is owed to him by the seller if the broker is authorized to do so. The $12,000 deposit held in the escrow account, due and payable now as commission earned, must be promptly withdrawn and transferred to the broker's business account or the broker could be found guilty of unlawful commingling. The principal broker could then use a portion of these funds to pay any referral fees or commissions due to a cooperating broker.

Closing attorneys who are not aware of this regulation, sometimes insist that the principal broker transfer all deposits to the closing attorney. The closing attorney then makes a check payable to the listing company and sometimes directly to the cooperating broker.

2.C.14 What procedures must the broker follow when the buyer and seller disagree as to how the deposit should be distributed?

Under certain conditions, the broker is authorized to release disputed earnest money without written consent. Examples include cases when the broker is in receipt of a final judgment of the court directing the disposition of the deposit or there is a final decision of a binding alternative dispute resolution. Another example is when a civil action is filed to determine the disposition of the earnest money at which time the broker may seek court authorization to pay the deposit into the court (an interpleader action).

The Department of Business Regulation has adopted new regulations (effective June 23, 2002) regarding how to handle deposit disputes. All deposits must be deposited into a principal broker's escrow account within five (5) days after the last signature of acceptance on a purchase and sales agreement. If the transaction does not close and the buyer and seller both claim the deposit, the following rules apply.

Disputed deposits must be transferred to the state treasurer, the general treasurer, by counting 180 days from the date that the funds were deposited into the listing company's escrow account. The funds must be transferred "promptly" after 180 days expired, so the transfer date will most likely be the 181st day after the funds were first deposited. A buyer and seller may agree to extend the 180-day period voluntarily in situations that may require more time, such as new construction or a property with a title problem.

Real estate licensees must send the buyer and seller a letter that includes mandatory language contained in the regulation at least 30 days before transferring the funds to the state treasurer. If the buyer and seller do not resolve their dispute after receiving the letter or agree to extend the 180 days, the licensee must complete a **Deposit Transmittal Form** and send a check to general treasurer with the deposit check with a copy to the Department of Business Regulation.

The general treasurer will not release the funds until he receives a **Claim for Return of Property** form. When the buyers and sellers provide the listing company with a mutual, written release, mediation agreement, arbitration award, or court order resolving the deposit dispute, the listing company must complete the **Claim for Return of Property** form and have the buyers and sellers sign as claimants. The treasurer will transfer the funds to the principal broker who will disburse the funds to the correct party.

The forms are posted on the DBR Web site at www.dbr.state.ri.us/real_estate.html, or they can be obtained from the DBR.

2.C.15   *What is an example of the situation just described?*

For example, the buyer's home doesn't sell by March 3rd and therefore, a written request for the return of the buyer's deposit money is initiated. The seller for no valid reason decides not to cooperate and refuses to sign the written release form. At this point, the broker is allowed to make a good faith decision that the contingency (the subject to sale) has not been met and initiate the return of the $2,000 deposit to the buyer by serving a 30-day certified mail written notice to both parties. During the required 30-day waiting period, the seller could take legal action to prevent the broker's good faith decision from happening.

2.C.16   *How soon do buyers get their earnest money back when they withdraw their offer before it was accepted?*

Obviously, a written release is not required when a seller rejects an offer or, before notification of acceptance by the seller of the offer, the buyers withdraw their offer. In both events, the deposit should be returned to the buyer without delay. In Rhode Island it is customary for licensees to keep deposit checks inside their transaction files until the seller accepts the buyers' offer. If the offer does not result in a contract, then the earnest money check is simply returned to the buyer or tenant.

2.C.17   *Can the broker take his or her commission money from the deposit directly out of the escrow account when the buyer and seller agree, just before closing, to rescind the contract? The broker feels that he or she did, in fact, earn the commission.*

A broker may pay his commission from the escrow account only if he or she has been authorized to do so.

For example, a seller accepts an offer for the sale of their home accompanied by a $2,000 deposit check. After acceptance, the buyers asked the seller to let them out of the contract due to an unexpected job transfer. The owner agrees and tells the buyers they can have their deposit back too. In this case, when the seller accepted the buyers' offer, a commission was earned; however, the listing broker cannot hold the buyers' and seller's deposit hostage. The broker must return the deposit as directed and look to the seller for compensation for services rendered.

2.C.18 *May property management funds, i.e., security deposits, be handled differently?*

Security deposits are expressly exempt from the DBR deposit requirements. Oddly enough, Rhode Island law does not require security deposits to be held in escrow accounts.

D. Fair Housing in Rhode Island

2.D.1 *What state agency is responsible for enforcing Rhode Island's fair housing laws?*

The Rhode Island Human Rights Commission enforces the Rhode Island Fair Housing Practices Act. The mission of this commission is to eliminate discrimination in Rhode Island and to establish equality and justice for all persons within the state through civil rights enforcement, advocacy, and education.

More information may be obtained from the Rhode Island Civil Rights Commission at:

Human Rights Commission
180 Westminster Street – 3rd Floor
Providence, RI 02903
Phone: (401) 222-2661
Fax: (401) 222-2616

2.D.2   Is the Rhode Island fair housing law similar to the federal fair housing laws?

Rhode Island fair housing laws recognizes more protected classes than federal law and applies to more property than federal law. Protected classes in Rhode Island include the same seven as the federal law, which are

1. race,
2. color,
3. religion,
4. sex,
5. country of ancestral origin,
6. familial status, and
7. disability (handicap).

Rhode Island protected classes also include the following:

- Sexual orientation, gender identity or expression
- Marital status
- Age
- Victims of domestic abuse

2.D.3   How is sexual orientation and/or gender identity defined?

Including sexual orientation as a protected class is intended to assure the basic human rights of persons to hold and convey property and to give and obtain credit, without regard to his or her sexual orientation. The term "sexual orientation" is defined as having or being perceived as an orientation for heterosexuality, bisexuality, or homosexuality. Basically, it describes the status of persons and does not confer legislative approval and does not impose any duty on any religious organization. The term "gender identity or expression" includes a person's actual or perceived gender, whether that identity, self-image, appearance, or expression is different from that traditionally associated with the person's sex at birth.

2.D.4   Who are victims of domestic abuse and how are they protected?

It is now illegal for landlords to refuse to rent to victims of domestic abuse, i.e., battered wives or to evict them because they are abused (based on their protected class status). However, the landlord may proceed with an eviction action against a tenant who fails or refuses to take reasonable steps to prevent disturbances of other residents or neighbors. In other words, if the tenant-victim lets the abuser return without calling the police, pursuing a restraining order, etc., the landlord may seek to evict the tenant.

Landlords cannot refuse to rent to families with children if their motivation is to avoid lead paint lawsuits, noise from children, damage by children, etc., unless they meet one of the special exemptions that are listed below. These exemptions are different from the federal ones:

- Owner-occupied two-family property;
- Owner-occupied two-family, three-family, or four-family property in which one of the units is currently occupied by a senior citizen or "infirm" (ill or disabled) person for whom children would cause a provable hardship.

E.   Megan's Law in Rhode Island

2.E.1 Are real estate agents under any obligations to comply with Megan's Law?

Briefly, Megan's Law requires that certain sex offenders, when released from prison, must register where they live with the local police. Rhode Island's version, Sexual Offender Registration and Community Notification, does not mention real estate licensees in particular. Thus, it appears that a real estate agent is not under obligation to discover or to disclose any information about the location of sex offenders.

3 Agency Overview

Brokerage involves bringing together two consumers, buyer and seller or landlord and tenant, to enter into a contract to sell, buy, rent, or manage real property in exchange for a fee. The state regulates the actions by the broker and his or her affiliated licensees who work with the consumer. Depending on the circumstance, the brokerage may work for a consumer-client or work with a consumer-customer.

Because the consumer relies on the real estate licensee for information, it is imperative that the consumer understands the type, if any, of the representation the consumer has with the real estate licensee. This chapter deals with agency concepts and disclosures, brokerage agreements, and antitrust laws.

A.   Agency Issues

3.A.1   How is agency defined in Rhode Island?

In real estate transactions, *agency* means a relationship in which a real estate broker acts for or represents another by the other person's **express** authority in a transaction. The relationship ("fiduciary relationship") is built on mutual respect, trust, honesty, and promise keeping. One party, called the client, **delegates authority** to his or her agent, who in return, **consents to act** for that client.

3.A.2   By what authority does the agent act?

In the case of a seller-client, the seller could elect to sell his or her home without the services of an agent but, instead, elects to **delegate** the task to an agent. The agent receives (from the seller) express **authority** to procure a buyer, and by **written authority** of the seller, the agent receives permission to put up a sign, use a lock-box system (in the owner's absence) to gain entry into the home, and to be present during offer negotiations. However, the agent does not have authority to bind the seller to an offer.

3.A.3   What is a special agency?

When the agent is hired to perform a specific task or transaction, a **special agency** is created. In the preceding scenario, the listing agent's authority is very limited. The listing agent is a *special agent,* that is, one who is hired for a short term and receives limited authority. Agency agreements spell out the agency relationship.

Even if all of the terms of the listing agreement are met, the seller's agent does not have legal authority to bind the seller to an excellent offer. In this case, even though a commission may have been earned, the seller's agent has no authority to bind the seller to the offer.

3.A.4   What is a general agency?

A *general agency* is created when the agent is empowered to represent the principal in a broad range of matters related to a particular business or activity. The general agent may, for example, bind the principal to any contract within the scope of the agent's authority.

A property manager is typically a general agent for the owner. Likewise, a licensee affiliated with the designated broker may be authorized to act as a general agent. The key terms are *long-term, broad authority.*

3.A.5   What is single agency?

In *single agency,* the agent represents only one party in any single transaction. The agent owes fiduciary duties exclusively to one principal, who may be either a seller-landlord or a buyer-tenant. Any third party is a customer. A customer is a consumer who is not being represented by a licensee but for whom the licensee may perform acts that do not rise to the level of representation.

A seller's agent is an agent who singularly **represents** the seller in a real estate transaction, sometimes referred to as the listing agent. The buyer is then considered the customer. A buyer's agent is an agent who singularly **represents** the buyer in a real estate transaction, who is often referred to simply as the buyer's agent. In buyer agency, the seller is the customer.

Rhode Island law presumes that all real estate licensees represent the seller unless there is an agreement to the contrary in writing, disclosed to "all parties." It is not required that the agreement be a buyer agency representation agreement. According to the Department of Business Regulation's interpretation, a buyer agency disclosure form is sufficient to fulfill this requirement.

Many real estate transactions in Rhode Island are single agency. The listing company represents the seller (seller's agent), and the cooperating broker represents the buyer (buyer's agent).

3.A.6   What is dual agency, and is it legal in Rhode Island?

Rhode Island law authorizes the use of **disclosed dual agency.** The practice is illegal without *informed, written authority.* Rhode Island prohibits undisclosed dual agency.

Disclosed dual agency is created when both a buyer and seller give their *written, informed consent* authorizing **one** licensee to represent both parties in the same transaction. Dual agency is becoming quite common in "in-house" transactions (i.e., one licensee in the company is an agent of the seller, another licensee of the company is an agent of the buyer, or one licensee is the agent of both the buyer and seller in one transaction). Rhode Island requires the real estate licensee to obtain the signatures of both the buyer and seller agreeing to the dual representation on a dual agency disclosure form, which must be incorporated in the purchase and sales agreements.

A real estate licensee who acts as a buyer's agent prior to becoming a dual agent must provide the buyer with a state-mandated agency disclosure form prior to the submission of an offer to purchase. The statute recommends that the form be given prior to qualifying a buyer or showing an appointment but only requires the form to be submitted prior to the offer. A listing agent prior to the creation of a dual agency agreement must provide the seller with a state-mandated agency disclosure form as part of the listing agreement.

3.A.7   What is nonagency, and is it legal in Rhode Island?

Rhode Island law does not specifically address the concept of a "nonagent" or "facilitator." By definition, nonagency is a situation in which a real estate licensee assists consumers without assuming the fiduciary duties of an agent.

As previously noted, Rhode Island law presumes that all real estate licensees represent the seller unless there is an agreement to the contrary in writing that must be disclosed to "all parties," which allows for the possibility of a nonagency relationship. However, Rhode Island law does not have an official "nonagency" disclosure form.

A "fee for service" relationship may offer nonagency possibilities, and a few companies in Rhode Island have begun to offer a "fee for service" menu. Theoretically, then, real estate licensees could assist sellers in a nonagency capability.

For example, a consumer may retain a real estate company to "lease" a For Sale sign or to advertise the property in the Statewide Multiple-Listing Service, Inc., without expecting the fiduciary duties of an agent. Some discount real estate firms offer little more than advertising in a multiple-listing service; the sellers show their own property, etc.; this also could be done theoretically as a "nonagent." However, typically these firms continue to disclose their status as being a seller's agent.

3.A.8   Who is the customer in a real estate transaction, and what duties does the agent owe the customer?

A *customer* is a consumer of real estate related services who is not being represented by the licensee. It is easy to recognize who the customer is when the agent represents the seller. The buyer is the customer. However, if the agent represents the buyer, the customer is the seller. Hence, it may be clearer to use the term *third party.*

While providing brokerage services to customers, licensees must do so **honestly** and **in good faith.** They must diligently exercise reasonable skill and care, and licensees must disclose all material adverse facts that the licensee knows except those material facts that have already been discovered or discussed. In addition, there is a duty to account for any customer's property that comes into the licensee's possession.

3.A.9   Who is the agent's client, and what does the agent owe this client?

A *client* is a party to a transaction who has an agency agreement with the licensee for brokerage services. Another name for a client is "the principal." The *principal* is the individual who hires and delegates authority to a broker to represent their interests. The principal can be the seller, landlord, buyer, or tenant.

3.A.10   What are an agent's duties and obligations?

Once an agency relationship is created, the licensee owes certain duties to his or her client in addition to the duties to a customer. Rhode Island rules of agency require the placement of the client's interest ahead of the interests of any other party to the transaction.

Agency duties are governed by common law (the rules established by tradition and court decisions) and statutory law (the laws enacted by state legislatures and governing bodies like the Rhode Island Department of Business Regulation). Additionally, today many courts also include duties defined in the National Association of REALTOR's Code of Ethics, even if the licensee is not a REALTOR.® The combination of these three defines the rights and duties of the parties. However, if the statutory rules conflict with the traditional laws of agency, then the rules supercede tradition.

In Rhode Island, the agent is obligated to place the client's interest ahead of the interest of any other party **(loyalty),** unless to do so violates the law. The Rhode Island agent must also **disclose** to the client all information known by the licensee that is material to the transaction and which is not known to the client or could not be discovered by the client through a reasonably diligent inspection. The agent must also disclose any financial interests the brokerage has in the transaction. The agent must fulfill the instructions **(obedience)** within the scope of the agency agreement (unless they are unlawful instructions). Finally, the Rhode Island broker may not accept any fees from more than one party to a transaction without disclosure to both parties.

When a seller's agent uses his or her superior skill to help the seller arrive at a realistic listing price, develop a marketing plan, and negotiate offers, **reasonable care** is demonstrated. A buyer's agent demonstrates **reasonable care** by helping the buyer evaluate property values, financial alternatives, offers and counteroffers.

The duty of **accounting** requires the recording and reporting of all funds received from or on behalf of the principal. State law requires too that these funds be deposited into a neutral escrow account maintained by the listing broker within five (5) banking days after the date on the document identifying receipt of the last signature of acceptance. Obviously, as mentioned earlier, unlawful *commingling* is illegal. (*Conversion* is the illegal practice of spending commingled funds for personal use.)

3.A.11 What acts may a licensee perform that are not client-level duties?

A licensee is allowed to perform some acts that require a real estate license for a consumer that are informative in nature and do not rise to client-level duties. Examples of such nonclient level care include responding to telephone inquiries, fielding questions at either an open house or the office, or setting appointments to view property. Other examples include accompanying an appraiser, inspector, or contractor on a visit to a property, completing factual information for a consumer on an offer, or referring a person to another broker or service provider.

3.A.12   Is seller subagency legal in Rhode Island?

Seller subagency is legally permitted in Rhode Island although an increasing number of real estate companies choose not to extend blanket or even extend any offers of subagency. The Statewide Multiple-Listing Service, Inc., regulations require listing contracts to contain a warning to sellers about the vicarious liability of involving subagents and provide a line for the seller to initial.

B.   Agency Disclosures

3.B.1   What is agency disclosure?

When representing parties in a real estate transaction, Rhode Island law requires listing agents and selling agents to provide written agency disclosures. The written disclosure form, signed by the client, verifies that the agent has, in fact, discussed agency options with the client. The law recommends that the disclosure form be given as soon as "practical" to a buyer, i.e., prior to qualifying a buyer or showing property by appointment as opposed to simply showing an open house. However, the agency disclosure form **must** be provided prior to submission of a written offer to purchase by a buyer.

It is important to note that just disclosing the broker's company policy does not create agency. The client must create an express agency relationship before the agent can provide specific assistance, a client-level activity that requires an agency agreement between the client and the agent.

3.B.2   What is "specific assistance"?

Rhode Island does not define "specific assistance" by statute or rule. However, in practical terms, it is a phrase often used to mean any communication beyond casual conversation that can lead to the discovery of confidential information. Usually specific assistance does not mean a casual open house showing or preliminary conversations concerning price range, location, and property styles, or responding to general factual questions concerning properties that have been advertised for sale or lease.

It means eliciting or accepting confidential information about someone's needs, motivation, or financial qualifications. With this knowledge, an unscrupulous agent could disclose the confidential information of a client to the other party in a real estate transaction, thereby compromising the client's bargaining position. This is why a licensee is required to discuss agency and to present the disclosure form as early as practical.

3.B.3 How is the disclosure made?

An agent working with a buyer must provide a state-mandated, written agency disclosure form to the buyer prior to the submission of a written offer to purchase. However, the law recommends that disclosure be made as soon as "practical," i.e., prior to qualifying a buyer or showing property by appointment. The licensee must provide a copy of the form to the listing agent at the time of showing. A listing agent must provide a state-mandated, written agency disclosure form to the seller as part of the listing agreement.

If the buyer or seller refuses to sign, the agent can complete the form and write down why the consumer refused to sign. The purchase and sales agreement must contain a state-mandated confirmation of the previously disclosed agency status of all real estate licensees who are involved in the process.

3.B.4 Do agency disclosures include agreements for broker compensation?

No, the obligation of either the seller or the buyer to pay compensation to a licensee is not determinative of an agency relationship. The broker's compensation is determined by a brokerage agreement, not by an agency disclosure form.

3.B.5 Does the agency disclosure create any obligations on the part of the buyer or seller?

The disclosure is simply an acknowledgment that agency has been discussed with the consumer. The consumer signs the document as "proof" that the licensee has discussed various agency options. Thus, signing of a disclosure form alone does not prevent the buyer or seller from working with other agents. However, it does create obligations on the part of the licensee/agent.

3.B.6 What is dual agency?

Many offices have a policy permitting dual agency, and the Rhode Island License Law allows dual agency **with informed written consent of the parties ("buyer-tenant and seller-landlord").** In a dual agency, the licensee must endeavor to remain impartial and not aggressively represent the interest of either party to the exclusion or detriment of the other party. Licensees can only act as dual agents with written consent of all the parties.

The possibility of dual agency should be discussed and agreed upon prior to the seller signing a listing agreement or before providing specific assistance to the buyer. If the consumer creates an agency agreement with the agent and agrees to the possibility of dual agency, then a second disclosure is required at the time that the agent actually becomes a dual agent.

When a buyer who is represented by a buyer's agent wishes to submit an in-house offer to a seller who is represented by a listing agent in the same firm, the agent must provide a state-mandated dual agency disclosure form to the parties for their signature.

3.B.7   What happens if no agency disclosure is made?

The agency disclosure law itself does not contain any penalties. However, failure to comply could constitute a real estate license law violation and could result in a lawsuit against a real estate licensee in addition to suspension or revocation of the agent's license.

3.B.8   Are any other disclosures required?

Unless a written notice to the contrary exists, licensees are prohibited from accepting undisclosed compensation (related to a transaction) from any person other than the agreed parties. Licensees must also disclose, in writing, any potential conflicts of interest.

Rhode Island License Law requires that all fees or commissions be paid directly to the employing broker. The broker then compensates the "salesperson" licensee for his or her participation in the transaction in accordance with the broker's written compensation policy. This policy is contained in the broker's written "Policy and Procedures Manual" as required by License Law.

C.   Brokerage Agreements

3.C.1   What is brokerage?

A real estate *broker* is defined as a person licensed to buy, sell, exchange, or lease real property for others and to charge a fee for those services. When a principal hires the broker to perform one of these services for a fee, the broker becomes that principal's agent. As discussed in the previous chapter, Rhode Island requires a license to comply with the license law, advertising one's services, negotiating, collecting rents, finding prospects, such as tenants or buyers, for real estate related activities.

3.C.2   What are brokerage agreements?

Brokerage agreements are essentially employment contracts requesting the professional services of the licensee, not the transfer of real estate. Brokers enter into independent contractor agreements with their affiliated licensees and "employment" contracts with sellers, buyers, landlords, and tenants. Brokerage agreements confirm compensation issues.

Depending on the agreement, the broker could be an agent or principal. In the independent contract with affiliated licensees, the broker is the principal and the affiliated licensees are the broker's agents. In a listing agreement, the seller is the principal (client) and the broker is the agent who "delegates" the work to his agents (affiliate licensees), who are subagents to the broker's agency relationship to the seller. In a brokerage agreement with a buyer, the buyer is the principal (client) and the broker is the agent, again "delegating" the work to his or her affiliates, who are subagents to the broker's agency relationship to the buyer.

3.C.3   What kind of agreement exists between a broker and the people who work for the broker?

The vast majority of affiliated licensees in Rhode Island are independent contractors. If a broker fails to provide his or her salesperson or associate broker with an independent contractor agreement, the broker could be liable for workers' compensation, unemployment, and the withholding of taxes. A Rhode Island law requires that principal brokers file a "notice of designation" for each affiliated licensee with the Department of Labor and Training or risk paying workers' compensation.

Brokers enter into independent contractor agreements with the licensees who work for the broker permitting the licensees to act as agents for the broker as subagents to the brokers principals. Thus, even though a salesperson or associate broker may negotiate the listing or buyer brokerage agreement, the agreement is in the name of the broker.

A broker is responsible for supervising the real estate activities performed by a salesperson or broker associate associated with the broker as a representative of the broker, even if the affiliate license is classified as an independent contractor. The salesperson or associate broker is responsible for keeping the employing broker fully informed of all activities being conducted on behalf of the broker and any other activities that might impact on the broker's responsibilities.

The principal broker must pay affiliated licensees their share of the commission within ten days after the broker receives it. The principal broker must also create a written termination policy to address the division of commissions after a licensee leaves his office.

3.C.4   Are referral fees legal in Rhode Island?

Every year real estate agents help buyers by referring them to other licensees across the United States. In return for the referral, a percentage or other agreed upon fee is paid to the referring broker. These fees are legal if paid between brokers.

3.C.5   What are the brokerage agreements between the brokerage and consumers?

A brokerage agreement sets forth the rights and obligations of both parties, and generally includes an agreement for broker compensation. These agreements are entered into by the brokerage with sellers, buyers, tenants, and landlords. The rules are the same whether the real estate is residential, commercial, industrial, or special purpose.

3.C.6   What are the various brokerage employment agreements with consumers?

A seller hires a broker under a **listing** agreement. An agreement between a broker and a buyer is a **buyer brokerage** agreement. A **management** agreement is a contract between a property owner and the broker who is hired to manage the rental property.

Even if an affiliate salesperson or associate broker negotiates the agreement, the contract is still between the consumer and the broker. It is important to remember that the agency disclosure merely acknowledges disclosure; the aforementioned agreements address exclusivity and compensation issues.

3.C.7   What are exclusive-right-to-sell listings?

Exclusive-right-to-sell listing agreements give brokerage firms the *exclusive right* to market the seller's property and receive during the term of the listing a commission regardless of which person sells it, including the owner. A variation is the *exclusive-agency listing,* in which the owner of the property promises to compensate a broker for locating a buyer, but the owner reserves the right to produce the buyer without paying the broker a commission. Rhode Island Rules state that the listing agreement must clearly state if the agreement is an exclusive-agency or exclusive-right-to-sell.

3.C.8   What is a net listing, and why is it illegal in Rhode Island?

A *net listing* is an agreement that specifies a net sale price to be received by the owner with the excess over that price to be received by the broker as commission. This situation presents a potential conflict of interest for the broker.

Often, the seller only realizes the true value of the property when an offer to purchase is obtained. Because of the appearance of impropriety between the fiduciary broker-client relationship and the broker's profit motive, the taking of a net listing is considered unprofessional conduct and constitutes a violation of Rhode Island General Laws and is specifically prohibited by Rhode Island License Law.

3.C.9   What specifically must a listing agreement include?

To have legal recognition, all listing contracts in Rhode Island must be written. The listing agreement must properly identify the property and the terms and conditions under which the property is to be sold.

Specifically, the listing agreement must include the listing price, the commission to be paid, the signatures of all concerned parties, and a definite expiration date. The requirement for a specific termination date effectively prohibits automatic renewal clauses in listing contracts. Agents are required to give a legible copy of the agreement to the owner as soon as reasonably practical after the listing agreement has been signed by the owner(s) and no later than ten days after all signatures to the agreement are obtained.

3.C.10   At what time may a listing broker place a For Sale sign on the property?

It is illegal to place a sign on any property offering it for sale, rent, or lease without the owner's consent. Thus, the broker may place the sign **whenever** the seller agrees. Many brokerages include specific authorization for a For Sale sign as part of the listing agreement.

3.C.11   Who or what determines the brokerage fee?

Any commission or fee in any brokerage agreement is fully negotiable among the parties to that brokerage agreement. The listing contract must spell out the broker's commission rate. It is typically a percentage of the sale or a flat fee.

Once the parties to a brokerage agreement agree on the structure of the commission, other than the listing agent, no party is allowed to alter or attempt to alter the commission arrangement without the prior written consent of the seller and listing agent. A licensee is prohibited from inducing a party to breach a contract in order to enter into a new contract that is motivated by the licensee's personal gain. The seller, in the listing contract, may authorize the listing company to share compensation with other licensees (cobrokerage), including a buyer's agent solely representing the buyer.

3.C.12   What is procuring cause?

Procuring cause in a real estate transaction means that a licensee started or caused a chain of events that resulted in the sale of a listed property. Procuring cause disputes happen between cooperating brokers and are normally settled by arbitration through local boards or associations. The Department of Business Regulation specifically does not have jurisdiction over disputes between brokers as to fees and commissions.

From time to time, a listing agent may feel that he or she did, in fact, earn a commission even though the transaction did not close (a procuring cause issue). Rhode Island case law does not require a closing to take place in order for a broker to earn a commission. In this situation, the listing agent may pursue the claim in court (but not through the Department of Business Regulation).

3.C.13   Are there any other considerations that may be included in a listing agreement?

In addition to the requirements mentioned in **3.C.9,** a licensee must specify a definite termination date that is not subject to prior notice and cannot advise against the use of an attorney in a real estate transaction including to review the listing contract. The listing agreement must state whether it is an exclusive-agency or exclusive-right-to-sell.

3.C.14   Who must sign a listing agreement?

To have a valid listing agreement, everyone who has an ownership interest should sign the listing agreement. For example, if a deed is held in the names of a husband and wife, both must sign the listing agreement. This is particularly important in transactions involving probate, property held in trusts or by corporations, and situations in which a husband and wife are in the process of divorcing.

Anyone who is authorized by the principal broker may sign the listing agreement on behalf of the brokerage. Ideally, the principal broker would sign all listing agreements, but many firms allow salespeople and associate brokers to sign.

3.C.15   What is a protection clause, and whom does it protect?

A *protection clause* protects the broker from unscrupulous sellers or buyers who take the broker's generated leads and then buy or sell the property *after the listing agreement expires* to avoid paying a commission to the broker. The protection period does not need to be part of the original contract; it could be an addendum or other document that is subsequently executed by both the seller and listing broker.

In Rhode Island, the broker is entitled to a commission for a transaction entered into by any buyer who saw the property while the contract was in effect. However, the protection period ends, in the typical contract, if the property is relisted with another broker.

Less common are exclusions, which typically are **not** mentioned in the initial listing contract. A listing agent may negotiate with the seller to exclude a named prospect from a listing agreement that the seller signs with a new agent after the agreement with the first agent expires.

For example: Seller agrees to compensate ABC Realty if Mary Smith or Bob Smith of 123 Elm Street, Providence, RI, purchases the property. Even if the seller agrees, the new broker may not agree to the exclusion or the seller never bothers to mention it until too late.

The worst case scenario for the seller is that he or she could owe two full commissions to both broker #1 and broker #2. In reality, the brokers often work out an arrangement with each other to split the commission equitably.

3.C.16   Can a broker solicit another broker's listing?

Rhode Island law prohibits a real estate licensee from soliciting another firm's listing. It is also illegal to induce a party to a contract to break the contract for the licensee's personal gain. The licensee may discuss other real estate services such as property management, insurance, etc., or the terms under which they could enter into a listing agreement after the current agreement with a competitor expires.

Legally binding listing agreements must be respected by outside parties. Alienating those involved in contractual relationships is illegal. According to Rhode Island license law, licensees are not allowed to negotiate or enter into listing agreements if it is known that the owner has an existing written, unexpired exclusive-right-to-sell or exclusive-agency listing agreement. Simply stated, agents are not allowed to solicit listings that have not been terminated with another brokerage.

However, from time to time, a seller who is under contract with a broker may contact a second broker and want to discuss listing with the second broker. The second broker may talk with a seller who initiates the call. However, any listing entered into cannot become effective until the first listing expires or is otherwise terminated.

3.C.17   Can a broker assign a listing to another broker?

Listing agreements may not be assigned, sold, or otherwise transferred to another broker without the express written consent of all the parties to the original agreement.

3.C.18   Is it legal for a salesperson who decides to work for a different broker to take several listings to the new brokerage?

Upon the termination of employment, licensees are not allowed to take or use any written brokerage agreements secured during their employment with the first broker. Brokerage agreements are the property of the principal broker and can be cancelled only by the broker and the seller, unless the terms of the contract state otherwise.

3.C.19   What must brokerage agreements with a buyer include?

Buyer agency agreements must be in writing. Rhode Island law presumes that all real estate licensees are seller's agents unless there is a written agreement to the contrary between buyers and sellers which is disclosed to all parties. Also, a law known as "the statute of frauds" requires a promise to pay a commission "for or upon the sale of any interest in real estate" to be in writing to be enforceable.

Agents in Rhode Island tend to use the agency disclosure form to satisfy the requirement that they are buyer's agents not seller's agents. Unfortunately, very few agents use written buyer agency agreements to establish their duties, commissions, and the termination date of the contract.

Rhode Island law does not specifically address additional terms of a buyer brokerage agreement. However, by considering the requirements for a listing agreement with a seller, it would appear that the buyer's brokerage agreement should include the broker's authority to assist the buyer in locating for purchase, lease, or other acquisition, real property identified during the term of the agreement. Compensation and cooperation with other brokers should be addressed.

Besides this buyer-client, other potential buyers that the agent is working with may be interested in the same property. The brokerage agency agreement terms should clarify how the buyer's agent may also represent those other buyers as well, regardless if the situation arises prior to, during, or after the end of the contract. Again, in looking at the requirement for preserving confidentiality with sellers under the buyer brokerage agreement, the licensee should not disclose to either buyer the terms of the other's offer. The agreement should discuss methods of contacting competing buyers.

Also in the terms of the agreement, the broker should ask the buyer to acknowledge that the licensee is solely acting as an agent, and not as an attorney, tax advisor, lender, appraiser, surveyor, structural engineer, property inspector, consultant, or other professional advisor. Buyers are advised to seek professional advice concerning the condition of the property, status of title, and other legal and tax matters concerning any proposed transaction.

3.C.20 Can a buyer's brokerage agreement be assigned or sold to another broker?

Unless the terms of the agreement state otherwise, buyer brokerage contracts cannot be assigned, sold, or otherwise transferred to another broker without the express written consent of all parties to the original agreement.

3.C.21 Can the licensee take his buyer brokerage agreements to the new broker if the licensee leaves the first broker to go to work for a second broker?

Upon termination, licensees are not allowed to take or use any written buyer brokerage agreements secured during their employment. These agreements remain the property of the principal broker and may only be cancelled by the broker and the buyer-client.

3.C.22 Does the agent owe the buyer-client anything after the termination of the relationship?

Legal and ethical implications of agency and certain duties of agency, such as confidentiality, may survive even after the termination of a buyer's agreement. Examples include accounting for monies and property related to and received during the contractual period as well as keeping confidentially requested information confidential.

3.C.23 Under what circumstances may a broker (or his or her agents) meet another broker's client?

Listing agents must allow buyer's agents to accompany prospects at any step in a real estate transaction, EXCEPT a listing agent is not required to permit a buyer's agent to be present when presenting an offer to a seller-client or discussing confidential matters with the seller-client. With the listing agent present, sometimes buyer's agents are afforded the courtesy to personally present their client's purchase agreement directly to the seller. If this courtesy is not extended, the buyer's agent present the buyer's offer or purchase agreement to the listing agent, and then the listing agent (singularly) presents the offer to the seller.

3.C.24   Do brokers have to cooperate and compensate each other?

Brokers recognize that while one brokerage has the listing, another broker may already be working with a buyer. The buyer wants to continue to work with his own agent, not the listing agent. In this situation, the seller benefits from the listing broker agreeing to share the compensation with the other broker who actually procures the buyer.

This cooperation benefits the seller by opening the property to more potential buyers. Rhode Island law does not require that the broker must cooperate with or compensate another broker. However, the listing agreement must include a statement disclosing the brokerage policy on cooperating with and compensating other brokerages whether the brokerage is acting as subagent or the other parties' agent, including whether the brokerage intends to share the commission with another brokerage. This disclosure is intended to inform the client of any policy that would limit the participation of any other brokerage.

3.C.25   What is a management contract?

Rhode Island does not have any specific rules regarding management contracts. By definition, a management contract is between the brokerage and the property owner who wishes to lease real property but does not want to deal directly with tenants and the property. The owner hires a real estate licensee to "manage" the property, i.e., locate tenants, handle repairs, collect rents, and so forth.

3.C.26   How are the owner's funds treated?

R.I.G.L. § 34-18-19, which governs security deposits, does not require owner's funds to be deposited in an escrow account. Security deposits are specifically exempt from the DBR deposit regulations. The broker must maintain records for three years.

D.   Antitrust Laws

3.D.1   Does Rhode Island have an antitrust law?

Yes, Rhode Island has its own antitrust law, which is known as "The Rhode Island Antitrust Act."

The stated purpose of the Rhode Island Antitrust Act is to complement federal antitrust laws. The act prohibits conduct such as price fixing, division of the market, and attempts to establish a monopoly, and it imposes penalties of up to $50,000 per offense in addition to injunctive relief.

4 Contracts and Closings Overview

When preparing to make and accept offers for the sale or rental of real property, buyers and sellers want to make decisions based on full knowledge of the property and title. Additionally, in today's marketplace, the real estate industry has seen a movement from *caveat emptor (buyer beware)* to seller disclosure. Today, sellers are asked to disclose information material to a buyer in order to allow the buyer to make an informed decision.

The Rhode Island General Laws have addressed these concerns. This chapter discusses disclosures covered by the Real Estate Sales Disclosure form, stigmatized properties, and certain environmental topics. It also considers contract issues including offers and acceptances and fraud. Closing concerns, including abstracting, and conveyance taxes are also discussed.

A.   Contract Issues

4.A.1   What is a contract?

A *contract* is a set of legally binding promises between two informed parties that must be performed and for which, if a breach occurs, the law provides a remedy. For legal recognition, all contracts related to the transfer of real estate in Rhode Island must be in writing pursuant to a law known as the "statute of frauds."

In Rhode Island, upon execution of any instrument in connection with a real estate transaction, licensees are required as soon as practicable to deliver legible copies of the original document to each party. It is the responsibility of the licensee to prepare sufficient copies of such instruments to satisfy this requirement.

4.A.2   What is the age of legal competence in Rhode Island, with no exceptions, to enter a contract?

In Rhode Island, a person is defined as legally competent at age 18.

4.A.3   What does "informed parties" mean?

Before entering into a legally binding contract to buy or sell real estate, the parties must offer and accept the same terms. Hence, sellers have a legal obligation to disclose important issues about the property so that both parties are informed. Otherwise, the buyer is buying less than agreed upon. It is an act of fraud to withhold disclosure of material adverse facts that are known by the seller or agent. In these situations, the buyer may be able to void the contract.

4.A.4   What are "deficient conditions?"

In Rhode Island, **deficient conditions** are those conditions or occurrences that are generally recognized as being of such significance that they would affect either party's decision to enter into a contract. Included in this definition are those situations that significantly and adversely affect the value of a property and those situations that significantly reduce the structural integrity of a property. Also, any situation that presents a significant health risk to the occupants of the property would be considered a **deficient condition.**

4.A.5   What is fraud?

Fraudulent acts require intentional deception in such a way as to harm another person. Included in the definition are fraudulent advertising, making false statements about a property's condition, and intentional concealment of known facts. Such fraudulent acts are subject to license suspension or revocation.

4.A.6   What is negligence?

Misrepresentation or omission of pertinent facts does not have to be intentional to bring liability exposure. **Negligence** occurs when licensees *should have known* that incorrect statements were being relied upon as material fact.

4.A.7   Who is permitted to draw up real estate contracts?

The preparation of mortgages or deeds by a real estate licensee is not common practice although such preparations are permitted as an exemption from the "unauthorized practice of law" statute. At the present time in Rhode Island, certain real estate licensees may draft deeds, mortgages, leases, and agreements, such as purchase and sales agreements, in transactions negotiated by him or her. Eligible licensees include salespersons and brokers, a real estate corporation or its officers whose "principal source of income is his or its commissions or profits from his, her, or its selling or leasing real estate, or both, and who regularly maintains an office for that purpose."

The licensee's name and business address must appear on the document if it is recorded, i.e., a deed or mortgage. In actual practice, real estate licensees regularly prepare purchase and sales agreements, addenda, listing agreements, and leases by filling in the blanks of preprinted documents prepared by legally trained individuals. (REALTORS® typically use forms from the Rhode Island Association of REALTORS® or Statewide Multiple Listing Agreement in the case of listing agreements.)

4.A.8   What specifically may a broker NOT prepare?

In Rhode Island, real estate brokers should be cautious to avoid the charge of practicing law without a license. A real estate licensee may not prepare any document that is commonly prepared by an attorney, and does not meet the above definition, such as a will, affidavits of child support or spousal support, or documents necessary to correct title defects. Licensed attorneys must be used for drawing up these documents.

4.A.9   How is property described in Rhode Island legal documents?

Property is described in metes and bounds, i.e., 1250 feet NW to Thatcher Brook; 580 westerly, etc., or and in conjunction with survey of Lot and Block. Descriptions are referenced by book and page number of the deed as opposed to by plats, as is more common in other states.

4.A.10   Is a legal description required in a listing agreement?

There must be a *meeting of the minds* to make a contract, and the street address must be definitive enough to clarify as to what is being purchased. Street addresses are not considered legal descriptions because of their temporary nature. A street address may be sufficient in a listing agreement or offer to purchase, but it is best that the legal description appear in a purchase and sales agreement to ensure a legally binding contract.

4.A.11   What forms must be completed during a real estate transaction?

In addition to the purchase and sales agreement, Rhode Island requires an agency disclosure form. A seller property disclosure is required prior to the buyer signing an offer to purchase. A lead-based paint disclosure form is required for transfers of all residential properties except for those with a lead-free certificate or that meet other exemptions from state regulations. Smoke and carbon monoxide detector certificates must be recorded with the deed at the time of transfer.

B.   Seller Property Condition Disclosure

4.B.1   What is the purpose of the seller property disclosure?

The purpose of the property disclosure is to forewarn prospective buyers of the condition of the property before writing an offer. If the procedures are not followed, then the buyer can revoke the offer.

The disclosure statement must include information about the condition of the following:

- Plumbing, electrical, and heating systems
- Any significant structural defects
- Presence of pests
- Radon
- Wastewater disposal systems
- Zoning information
- Whether the property is located near wetland

State law requires certain minimal mandatory language, but real estate licensees and sellers are free to disclose additional information if desired. No particular language is required for the disclosure of specific items as long as the required disclosure items are addressed.

4.B.2   When must the property disclosure be made?

A property disclosure completed by the seller must be provided to and signed by the prospective buyer prior to the presentation of the buyer's offer to the seller by the real estate licensee.

4.B.3   To what properties does the seller property disclosure apply?

Rhode Island's seller property disclosure is required if the property has at least one but not more than four dwelling units. The disclosure must also be made for vacant land even if transferred by a builder or developer. It does not apply to transfers of commercial and industrial properties and five or more residential units. Even for residential properties, there are certain exemptions.

4.B.4   What transactions are exemptions to the disclosure form requirement?

Some property owners and/or transactions are exempt by law. Major exempt transactions include a transfer by

- a builder or developer of a new, unoccupied dwelling unit;
- a lender;
- the state;
- a guardian, conservator, trustee, or other fiduciary;
- relocation companies;
- court order, i.e., divorce, bankruptcy;
- intrafamily transfers; and
- transfer with no consideration paid.

Additional potential exemptions may be found in the Rhode Island General Laws.

4.B.5   Who must make the property disclosure?

The seller, unless exempt, has a legal obligation to complete, sign, and deliver the property disclosure to prospective buyers, the listing agent, buyer's agent, and/or seller's subagents with whom the buyer is working.

4.B.6   What are the consequences if the disclosure is not made or is made after the offer has been accepted?

If the seller or agent does not deliver the disclosure statement in a timely manner, a buyer may withdraw his or her offer or revoke its acceptance **without liability,** within three (3) days following personal delivery of the statement or five (5) days if delivered by mail. If the disclosure is not made before closing, seller may be liable for damages.

4.B.7   How should changes be made after the seller filled out the disclosure form?

The seller has an obligation to update the seller property disclosure form. If a "materially deficient condition" changes or is discovered after the signing of an offer but prior to the signing of a purchase and sales agreement, the buyer may terminate or renegotiate the offer.

If a "materially deficient condition" changes or is discovered **after** the signing of a purchase and sales agreement, the buyers may terminate the contract and receive a full refund of their deposit. Or, the buyer can provide the seller with an inspection report, i.e., home, pest, radon, septic, etc., and allow the seller an opportunity to decide about making repairs. The seller must then notify the buyer within seven (7) days after receiving the inspection report as to whether the seller will cure the defect. The statute allows for delays in completing the inspection, etc.

4.B.8   What are the licensee's responsibilities to ensure that the seller makes the disclosure and that the buyer receives it in a timely fashion?

The law requires that every purchase and sales agreement contain an acknowledgment that the buyer has seen the Real Estate Sales Disclosure form. The seller or real estate agent can be fined for failure to comply with this requirement or the lead inspection disclosure requirement described above.

4.B.9   What if the property transfers without a seller disclosure statement?

A transfer is not invalidated nor is a defect in title created solely because of a failure of a person to comply with the written disclosure requirement. The exception occurs if the purchase and sales agreement fails to include the lead inspection disclosure, or the seller fails to provide the buyer with copies of any lead inspections that have been performed on the property. In either of these situations, the buyer has the right to void the purchase and sales agreement by giving written notice to the seller prior to the closing.

4.B.10   Whose signatures must be on the disclosure form?

Anyone whose name appears on a deed must sign the seller disclosure form. For example, if the husband and wife are both on the property title, both sellers must sign the form. Agents risk increasing their own legal liability by signing a disclosure form on behalf of a seller and are strongly discouraged from doing so.

State law requires that at the time of the listing, the licensee obtain a completed disclosure signed and dated by each seller. When the disclosure is delivered to the buyer, the licensee is legally required to obtain the signatures of all buyers and the date of signature.

The sellers disclose that the provided information regarding the property's condition is based on information actually known by them and certify that the information is true and accurate to the best of their knowledge. The buyers acknowledge receipt of the document but note that the document is not intended to be a warranty or a substitute for any inspection deemed necessary by the buyer. If there is more than one buyer, any one buyer may accept delivery of the executed statement.

4.B.11 What if the buyer will not sign the disclosure document?

Rhode Island law requires the buyer to sign that he has received the disclosure document and makes no provision for a buyer's refusal to sign. Given that home inspection contingencies in a purchase and sales agreement typically provide that a buyer may terminate the agreement only if his or her home inspection uncovers substantial or material, deficient conditions that were not disclosed in the seller disclosure form, the buyer would harm himself by not signing the disclosure form.

C.   Offers and Acceptances

4.C.1 Must the listing agent let the buyer's agent present the offer to the seller-client?

By Rhode Island law, listing agents are not required to permit a cooperating broker to be present when presenting offers or discussing confidential matters with their seller-clients. However, Multiple-Listing-Service rules allow a cooperating broker to attend the presentation of his buyer-client or customer's offer to the seller unless the seller refuses.

4.C.2 In what order are multiple offers presented to the seller for consideration?

Rhode Island law states that any and all offers received by a listing agent must presented to the seller for consideration prior to the signing of a purchase and sales agreement or the listing broker can face disciplinary action. The seller must be permitted to view all offers to determine which offer is best for the seller. While Rhode Island law does not expressly require a listing agent to formally communicate rejections, acceptances, counteroffers, etc., such timely communication is implied in agency laws.

Licensees need to help the buyer understand that another offer may be presented while the seller is considering the first offer. No particular courtesies are extended to the person writing the first offer, and a seller has no legal obligation to accept the highest offer or any offer.

4.C.3 Should subsequent offers be presented to the seller if the seller has already accepted an offer?

As a matter of practice, listing agents may present backup offers while contingencies, such as home inspection or finance contingencies are still in effect, but the listing agent does not have a legal requirement to do so. Also, listing agents will present (voluntarily) offers if a Hubbard clause is in effect. (A Hubbard clause in a purchase and sales agreement makes the transaction subject to the sale of the buyer's existing home. If another buyer makes an offer, the first buyer will have a period of time, such as 48 hours, to waive the Hubbard clause or risk losing the property to the second buyer.)

Neither state law nor the standard Rhode Island listing contract require the agent to continue to present offers after one has been accepted. However, some sellers want to continue to see offers that arrive even after the seller has accepted an offer. The seller is still bound to the first accepted offer but may wish to view a later offer as a possible backup or secondary offer, particularly during key stages of the transaction, i.e., during the home inspection or prior to the buyers obtaining a loan commitment letter.

4.C.4   Once the offer is accepted, what rights does the buyer have in the property?

After a purchase agreement is signed, and the buyer or buyer's agent is in receipt of the signed document, equitable title passes to the purchaser. At this point, the buyer has an insurable interest in the property and is allowed the opportunity to purchase additional insurance. The seller cannot arbitrarily withdraw his acceptance and sell to another party.

4.C.5   What if the buyer and seller agree to a sales price that is different from the one submitted to the lender?

In this scenario, the buyer (and seller) would be submitting a false purchase agreement. One of the offers is used **to purchase** the property (from the seller) while the other is used **to finance** the property. In such fraudulent cases, the offer to purchase can be either written or just an oral arrangement while the offer to finance is generally written.

Thus, the true purchase price is known only between the contracting parties. The purpose of these contracts is to enable the buyer *to obtain a larger loan* than the true sales price or to enable the buyer *to qualify for a loan* which the buyer otherwise could not obtain. *Thus, the lender is deceived.* In Rhode Island, a real estate licensee who violates this law would be subject to disciplinary action.

4.C.6   How soon must a buyer's deposit (if any) be deposited into an escrow account?

Rhode Island license law requires a real estate licensee to deposit escrow funds once a purchase and sales agreement has been executed. (In the parts of Rhode Island where a two-step, offer and purchase and sales agreement process is common, a broker would typically deposit the funds once the offer is signed.) A new license regulation requires an escrow agent to deposit a buyer's deposit within five days after he or she receives the funds from the buyer or cooperating broker.

4.C.7   Are there any other requirements of a real estate licensee?

Rhode Island license law requires a real estate licensee to deliver copies of listing agreements, leases, purchase and sales agreements, and related agreements, such as addendum, to all signatories of the agreement at the time of execution (signing).

D.   Closings

4.D.1   Under what circumstances may the buyer request that some funds be withheld from the seller until all of the repairs are completed?

Matters related to performance of the seller or buyer are most often legal judgments requiring the professional expertise of an attorney. If a buyer demands the withholding of funds as a matter of right and refuses to perform unless the demand is met, the buyer may likewise be liable for a failure to perform if the buyer's demand is not within the scope of the appropriate law governing the circumstances. The real estate licensee should strongly urge their buyer-client to consult with an attorney before making such demands.

If, however, the buyer and seller freely negotiate the withholding of funds for repairs that are required by the purchase and sales agreement or otherwise acknowledged by the seller as requiring completion or if the seller has failed to remove all of his belongings or leave the house in "broom clean" condition, the real estate licensee can assist in the negotiation and request an appropriate party hold an escrow. The wisest choice as an escrow agent is usually the closing attorney who is familiar with these arrangements.

4.D.2   Who is responsible for the accuracy of a closing?

The closing attorney and/or the parties themselves are responsible for the accuracy of closing documents, not the broker.

4.D.3   Can brokers charge to prepare some documents?

This issue is a murky area of law. Charging a fee to prepare certain documents may lead to charges of the unauthorized practice of law. Real estate licensees clearly have the right to fill in blanks in certain legally prepared documents as stated above, and no law specifically precludes them from charging for this service. However, the law contemplates that this service is performed as part of a real estate transaction negotiated by the licensee. If these services are unbundled in a "fee for service" business model where the buyer and seller negotiate their own transaction, courts may be inclined to prevent licensees from charging for any services interpreted as the unauthorized practice of law.

4.D.4   Are there any other statements or documents of which to be aware?

Yes, a completed smoke detector/carbon monoxide detector certificate must be filed at the time the deed is recorded. The certificate verifies that the smoke and carbon monoxide detectors have been inspected by the local fire chief, are properly located, and are in good working order. Although the smoke detector requirement has been in effect for many years, the carbon monoxide detector law only went into effect in January 2002.

This is required in the transfer of new homes with

- gas utilities;
- property that has been converted to residential use with gas utilities; and
- all existing, single-family, two-family, or three-family homes regardless of their heating source.

This law does not exempt seasonal rentals even if they are unheated.

E.   Stigmatized Properties

4.E.1   What is a stigmatized property?

A *stigmatized* or psychologically impacted *property* is one that has acquired an undesirable reputation for a problem that is unrelated to a physical defect, such as a wet basement or termites. Stigmatized properties include those properties where a murder, suicide, or felony occurred or is suspected to have occurred.

4.E.2   Is there any responsibility for failure to disclose information about stigmatized property?

The essence of the issue is discovery not disclosure. There is no duty for the seller or the seller's agent to volunteer such information. However, nothing in the law permits the seller to misrepresent the situation or falsely deny that the condition exists if asked by a buyer.

Rhode Island case law has not yet imposed a duty to investigate or independently disclose information to a buyer. However, if the buyer's agent had prior knowledge, then under agency law, the buyer's agent may have a duty to disclose the known information.

Certain information may not be disclosed. Under federal fair housing laws, it is illegal to stigmatize a property in which someone with a medical condition such as human immunodeficiency virus (HIV) or someone diagnosed with acquired immune deficiency syndrome (AIDS) is rumored to have lived.

4.E.3   Are there any other special disclosure issues in Rhode Island?

A new law requires sellers of property that is served by a private water supply ·i.e., a well, to provide buyers with copies of any previous well testing results in the seller's possession and notify the buyer of any known problems with the well.

F.   Environmental Concerns

4.F.1   Who implements CERCLA in Rhode Island?

The Rhode Island Department of Environmental Management under state law administers CERCLA and its own assessment and cleanup programs at contaminated sites of state interest. DEM attempts to work with property owners under state law to avoid their inclusion on a federal list. In addition, states provide assistance to the EPA to clean up high-priority sites on the National Priority List (NPL) and to undertake site assessments for sites not yet on the NPL. For more information, contact the Office of Waste Management of the Department of Environmental Management at www.state.ri.us/dem/programs/benviron/waste/index.htm.

4.F.2   Who is responsible for cleaning up hazardous waste on a property?

Responsibility varies. Since clean-ups can be quite costly, prospective buyers should certainly obtain as many reports as available from the EPA, DEM, and even from private environmental specialists. On contaminated sites, Rhode Island's DEM can require the submission of a clean-up report or an action plan for cleaning up the property.

4.F.3 Where may a buyer go to learn more about wetlands protection?

Licensees should keep in mind that Rhode Island has many miles of coastline (hence, the nickname of the "Ocean State"). There are different requirements for fresh water wetlands and salt marshes. The primary regulatory entity is the Department of Environmental Management, Office of Water Resources. The Office of Compliance and Inspection is charged with enforcement.

4.F.4 What state agency controls rights to water in Rhode Island?

Rhode Island is a densely populated, largely urban state, so water rights are not as crucial as they are in the western states. The Department of Environmental Management, Office of Water Resources manages issues relating to surface, ground water protection, and wetlands. The Office of Water Resources is divided into Surface Water Protection and Groundwater and Wetlands Protection.

4.F.5 Are there other water-related issues?

Customarily, well testing is done in Rhode Island for bacteria and high levels of nitrate. A new law requires sellers to notify buyers that a private water supply must be tested in accordance with Rhode Island Department of Health regulations. Once regulations are promulgated, sellers of property that is served by a private water supply, i.e., a well, will be required to provide buyers with copies of any previous well testing results in the seller's possession and notify the buyer of any known problems with the well.

4.F.6 Of what should the buyer be aware before building on an acreage and installing a septic system?

In Rhode Island, state and municipal officials monitor septic tanks and private sewage disposal systems. For proper drainage, the ground must be able to absorb the liquid waste. A percolation test is conducted that monitors the time it takes water poured through a pipe to be absorbed by the soil. A permit may not be issued if there is insufficient absorption.

4.F.7   Are there other issues of which a developer should be aware?

Some towns and cities have local ordinances and bylaws that require septic systems known as ISDS and cesspools to be tested prior to transfer of real estate. Some also require special approval for septic inspections, which real estate licensees and developers should always make certain to check.

4.F.8   Does Rhode Island have a lead-based paint hazard reduction law?

Basically, Rhode Island operates under the federal Title X Lead-Based Paint Poisoning Prevention Act passed in 1992 with certain additions. Rhode Island law covers lead in the exterior of buildings and also soil. Also, vacant land and properties built after 1978 need not contain the lead inspection disclosure.

This law requires notification of the possible exposure of lead-based paint in all pre-1978 residential and apartment dwellings. The Rhode Island Department of Public Health (DOH) is the authority on lead-based paint issues; however, a new law will transfer some of DOH's authority to the Rhode Island Housing Resources Commission. In Rhode Island, both the Rhode Island Department of Health and the EPA have jurisdiction over lead-based paint disclosure enforcement.

The seller is required to notify the buyer of any known lead-based hazards and provide the buyer with any information on lead-based hazards from risk assessments or inspections in the seller's possession. The seller must also provide a booklet to the buyer or tenant that contains a special Rhode Island supplement. Buyers (but not tenants) have the right to have the property inspected within ten days or any agreed-upon time period, or the buyer may waive this right. Failure to disclose any known lead presence is subject to $10,000 fine per violation. Copies of these disclosures must be retained for three years.

A major new Rhode Island lead law was enacted in June 2002, which is expected to be phased in from 2002 to 2004. The law will require landlords to have their rental units periodically inspected, and all property owners to comply with new lead mitigation standards.

4.F.9   Does Rhode Island require any other disclosures of environmental presence, such as asbestos, UFFI, etc.?

Rhode Island law requires a seller of vacant land or a one-unit to four-unit residential dwelling to disclose in writing any deficient conditions of the property prior to presenting a buyer's offer to purchase to the seller. "Deficient conditions" include the presence of asbestos, radon, pests, underground storage tanks, issues surrounding a private well, septic system or cesspool, wetland, etc.

G.   Abstracting

4.G.1   Is Rhode Island a title or lien theory state?

Rhode Island is a modified lien-title theory state. This means that the owner-borrower gives the lender a mortgage lien to use as collateral instead of a deed. The lender has the owner-borrower sign a promissory note as evidence of the debt and sign a mortgage lien instrument as collateral for the debt.

If the owner defaults on the loan, the lender invokes the "Statutory Power of Sale Clause" contained in the mortgage and gives the borrower at least 30 days notice (in some cases a longer notice period is given) in which to cure the default. If the borrower does not cure the default within the notice period, legal title to the property automatically passes to the foreclosing lender. No court action is required for the lender to obtain title to the property. In Rhode Island, the owner-borrower never relinquishes legal title, provided the loan is paid in accord with the note.

4.G.2   How does a buyer know that title to the property is "good and marketable?"

The buyers and/or their lenders retain a title attorney to perform a title search of public records. In Rhode Island, the deeds and related documents that pertain to transfers of real estate are filed in the "land records" of the town or city where the land is located rather than in a county office as is common in larger states. If the records show that the current owner has an unbroken chain of title for 40 or more years, the owner's title is presumed to be a "marketable record title" to that interest, subject to easements, conservation restrictions, and other encumbrances.

4.G.3   Which party is responsible for searching public records?

The buyer normally assumes responsibility for performing a title search. If the buyer is financing the transaction with a mortgage, the lender must allow the buyer to select his or her own title attorney to perform the title search and to select the title insurance policy. Even in a cash deal, the prevailing practice is for buyers to arrange for their own title searches in order to obtain title insurance.

H.   Conveyance Taxes

4.H.1   What are conveyance taxes?

For increased revenue, Rhode Island charges property owners a transfer tax when they transfer legal title to their properties. Unless otherwise agreed upon by the buyer and seller, the seller is legally responsible for paying this tax, which was increased in July 2002, from $1.40 to $2.00 per $500 on most transfers of real estate.

Historically, Rhode Island used differing denomination stamps (postage size) to record the amount of the tax and affixed them to the deed. The stamps were then franked (defaced) to show that the tax had been paid. To the property owner, it was considered a transfer tax stamp. To the state of Rhode Island, it was considered a revenue stamp. To the recorder's office, it was considered a documentary stamp. In reality, it was the same thing looked at from three perspectives.

Today, Rhode Island just uses a receipt and affixes it to the deed for recordation. However, it is sometimes referred to as a revenue stamp; but it is not—it is a revenue tax.

4.H.2   How are conveyance taxes computed?

The Rhode Island conveyance tax is $2.00 per every $500 of sale price or fraction thereof. For example, here is how to compute the taxes on a $200,000 sale. $200,000 divided by $500 = 400 multiplied by $2.00 = $800.

Typically, at closing, unless otherwise agreed by the buyer and seller, the seller is legally responsible for paying this tax.

4.H.3   Are there any other taxes assessed during closing of which the licensee should be aware?

In a real estate transaction, the buyer has a legal duty to deduct and withhold a nonresident withholding tax to be paid to the Rhode Island Division of Taxation if the seller is not a resident of Rhode Island. The nonresident withholding tax is 6 percent of the total purchase price in most nonresident sales or 9 percent if the seller is a nonresident corporation. Typically, the closing attorney assumes the responsibility of seeing that the tax is collected.

5 License Law Enforcement Overview

This chapter covers how the Rhode Island Real Estate Commission considers violations of license law or rule. Generally, after proper disciplinary hearings, the Rhode Island Real Estate Commission exercises its control over licensees through public reprimands; reeducation; fines; and the denial, suspension, or revocation of licenses.

The Department of Business Regulation also requires two added protections to provide compensation to a consumer who suffers monetary damage as a result of a licensee's error or negligence. Each licensee is required to purchase errors and omissions (E&O) insurance that is similar to malpractice insurance and to contribute to a recovery fund.

A. License Law Enforcement

5.A.1 Is a violation of Rhode Island license law a misdemeanor or a felony?

Violation of state license law is a misdemeanor, which is punishable by imprisonment of a maximum of one year for a first offense; a maximum of two years for a second offense. Other penalties may include various fines, including administrative, and suspension or revocation of a license. The maximum fine for most violations of real estate license law is $1,000. In addition, any person who performs the acts of a real estate broker or salesperson without a license could face a fine of $100 to $500 and/or imprisonment for a maximum of one year if convicted for a first offense; additional offenses are punishable by a fine of $500 to $1,000 and/or imprisonment for a maximum of two years if convicted. Corporations face a fine of $1,000 to $2,000 for a first offense and $2,000 to $5,000 for additional offenses.

Also, if a licensee received any funds resulting from a violation of real estate laws, the DBR can order this licensee to pay a penalty as much as three times the amount of the funds. Finally, the DBR can also impose penalties against real estate schools for operating without a license.

5.A.2   *Under what circumstances may the Department of Business Regulation investigate licensees?*

The Department of Business Regulation processes complaints that are filed by the general public or other real estate licensees. The DBR can also act on its own to suspend or revoke a real estate license.

The Department of Business Regulation staff–namely, the Real Estate Administrator, handles investigations with the assistance of DBR attorneys, and the Associate Director of the Commercial Licensing and Regulation Division.

5.A.3   *What are some of the reasons that can trigger an investigation?*

The DBR is charged with protecting the interests of the public. Consequently, the commission has jurisdiction over actions by a licensee that can harm the consumer in a real estate transaction. Additionally, another agency, such as the Human Rights Commission may refer a complaint to DBR, e.g., if the Human Rights Commission finds that a broker or salesperson violated fair housing laws.

Under 5-20.5-14, the commission may investigate a licensee's actions for a number of reasons. Among those mentioned include any of the following reasons: fraudulent activities, substantial misrepresentations, undisclosed dual agency, accepting a commission as a licensee from anyone except the brokerage, and representing two brokerages without the knowledge of both brokers. Also, the DBR can revoke a real estate license if a broker or salesperson fails to comply with continuing education requirements, produce documentation of E & O insurance, or other renewal requirements.

The DBR may investigate a broker for other reasons: for failing to account for or remit monies into the broker's trust account in a timely manner, paying a referral fee (commission) to someone who is not licensed for real estate referrals, and for false or misleading advertising. Other reasons include failing to provide requested information to the real estate commission in a timely manner (within 14 days), or any other conduct that demonstrates deceit or professional incompetence, including habitual intoxication or the addiction to the use of drugs. The commission may act to discipline a licensee who has been convicted of forgery, embezzlement, obtaining money under false pretenses, bribery, larceny, extortion, conspiracy to defraud, or any similar offense or offenses, or pleading guilty or nolo contendere to any such offense or offenses.

As previously mentioned, Rhode Island rules prohibit dual contracts, posting a For Sale sign without the owner's permission, acting as undisclosed principal, and failing to maintain records for three years. All offers must be promptly presented. The broker must properly supervise his or her licensed salespeople and provide information in a timely manner when requested by the commission. A licensee must never advise against using the services of an attorney. The salesperson must promptly return to the broker any information and records when the salesperson terminates employment with the broker. The broker must notify the Director of DBR of the termination within ten days.

5.A.4   How does DBR determine when and if to follow up on a complaint?

If DBR acts on its own, it must notify a licensee in writing of its intended action, e.g., suspension, refusal to renew a license, etc., and grounds for the action, e.g., misrepresentation, failure to report all offers to the seller prior to signing a purchase and sales agreement, etc. The DBR reviews the complaint and then forwards the complaint to the licensee who must file an answer within 20 days. The DBR then returns the answer to the complainant and schedules a hearing after giving the parties 20 days' notice.

5.A.5   Under what circumstances may the investigating committee decide not to hold a hearing?

Although not formally stated in the statutes, if the DBR determines that there was no probable cause that warrants discipline, a letter is sent and the case closed. Reasons for refusing to set a hearing can include the triviality of the allegation, insufficient evidence, effort to solve on a local level, lack of clarity of the issue, and lack of jurisdiction.

Recall that the mission of DBR is to protect the public. Thus, DBR rules do not authorize DBR to consider or conduct hearings involving disputes over fees or commissions between cooperating brokers, salespersons, and other brokers.

5.A.6   How does the DBR decide on holding a hearing?

In determining the appropriate action, DBR considers not only the severity of the violation and the sufficiency of evidence but also the possibility that the problem could be better resolved by other means available to the parties, without DBR involvement. DBR considers the clarity of the laws and rules that support the alleged violation, the clarity of its jurisdiction, whether the violation is likely to recur, and the record of the licensee.

5.A.7   What time frames must be observed?

A written notice of a commission-conducted hearing, together with a statement of charges, is sent by certified mail to the licensee's last known business address, at least **20 days** before the scheduled contested case hearing. The notice of hearing gives the date, time and place of hearing, a statement that authorizes the presence of legal council, and their legal and jurisdictional authority. The DBR includes references to applicable statutes and rules along with a brief statement of the matter. The licensee may request a formal hearing by filing the request and answer to the charges within **20 days** after receiving them.

Similar time frames apply when someone other than the DBR files a written complaint. First, the DBR reviews the complaint and then forwards the complaint to the licensee who must file an answer within **20 days.** The DBR then returns the answer to the complainant and schedules a hearing after giving the parties **20 days'** notice. The DBR must render a written decision within **60 days** of the final hearing.

5.A.8   Can the respondent request a different hearing date?

Yes, written requests for a continuance may be considered if mutually agreeable to the parties or in the case of a legitimate problem such as major illness, death in the family, etc.

5.A.9   How may testimony be taken before the hearing?

Testimony may be taken by deposition compelling any involved party to appear and depose in the same manner as witnesses compelled to appear and testify in civil cases.

5.A.10   What are the legal effects of the hearing and possible disciplinary actions?

The DBR can exonerate the license, or revoke, suspend, or possibly not renew the license. Other disciplinary actions include probation, additional education or training, reexamination, issuing a citation and warning, or imposition of a civil penalty not to exceed $1,000.

5.A.11   What happens if the respondent does not appear?

The hearing will be held without the licensee. The licensee will be bound by the decision as if the licensee had been there. In other words, the licensee loses the right to cross-examine witnesses and to present the licensee's defense.

5.A.12 Is there any possibility of an appeal?

A licensee may appeal to the superior court in the jurisdiction in which he or she resides within 30 days from service of DBR's decision and post a bond of $1,000. The Administrative Procedures Act judicial review governs the process.

B. Suspended or Revoked Licenses

5.B.1 What are the immediate effects of a suspended or revoked designated broker's license?

A suspended or revoked license must be returned to the Department of Business Regulation and, as of the effective date, engaging in activities that require a license, is terminated. Note though, during the penalized period, a suspended or revoked licensee is allowed to receive compensation earned prior to the effective date of the suspension or revocation. If it is the broker's license that is suspended or revoked, all licensees must transfer their licenses to another office within ten days or return it to the DBR for cancellation.

5.B.2 What are the effects on brokerage agreements when the designated broker's license is suspended or revoked?

Upon receipt of the DBR decision, the suspended or revoked broker must cancel all listings and property management agreements. The seller or lessor must be apprised of their rights to list or lease with someone else. It is illegal to sell or assign listings or management agreements without written authorization of the seller or lessor.

A suspended or revoked broker licensee may not finalize any pending closings. With written approval of the concerned parties, this task must be delegated to a new entity that will handle the trust funds and close the transaction. Such entities can include another broker, an attorney, financial institution, or escrow company.

All advertising must be canceled. Suspended or revoked brokers are also prohibited from advertising real estate in any manner as a broker or answering their business telephone in any manner, which might indicate that the brokerage is active in the real estate business.

5.B.3 Is the designated broker disciplined if one of his or her licensees is disciplined?

Any unlawful act or violation by a licensee is not cause for the revocation of the broker's license unless the broker had actual knowledge of the unlawful act or DBR violation. Note though, during the penalized period, a suspended or revoked licensee is allowed to receive compensation earned prior to the effective date of the suspension or revocation.

C.   Errors and Omissions (E&O) Insurance

5.C.1   Does Rhode Island have a recovery fund for victims?

Yes, the Department of Business Regulation requires all real estate licensees to fund a real estate recovery fund. The purpose of the fund is to compensate consumers for acts that are often exempt from E & O insurance coverage or to protect them from licensees who are bankrupt and/or have no E & O insurance. The fund assists consumers who obtain a judgment against a real estate licensee for fraud, misrepresentation, or deceit resulting from a real estate transaction in which the licensee is involved in his or her capacity as a licensee.

To be eligible for payment, the consumer must first exhaust all remedies and collection procedures against the licensee. The maximum amount payable to the consumer from this fund is $50,000 per licensee found guilty of the cause of action. Real estate licensees cannot apply for reimbursement for an unpaid commission from this fund even if it resulted from fraud.

5.C.2   What is the fund's minimum balance, and how is it maintained?

A broker or salesperson is assessed a $25 fee for the fund which is due with the first initial license application. If the balance of the fund falls below $200,000 at the end of a calendar year, the Department of Business Regulation may assess a fee of $25 during the next license renewal cycle (every two years).

5.C.3   What time frames must be observed?

The claimant must file suit within two years of the accrual of the cause of action and notify DBR if the action could result in a claim against the fund. Following a court judgment in favor of the claimant, and after the exhaustion of all appeals, the claimant must request an order from the court to order DBR to pay the claim after giving ten days' advance notice to DBR. The claimant must show that he or she is not related to the licensee, has a judgment against the licensee, has complied with the statutory notice requirements, and made reasonable searches and investigations of the licensee's assets to no avail.

5.C.4 What is the effect on the licensee if payment from the fund is made?

If a payment is made from the fund, the DBR automatically revokes the real estate licensee's license. The broker or salesperson is prohibited from obtaining a new licensee until he or she repays the amount in full and 12 percent interest. This applies even if the licensee obtains a bankruptcy discharge.

5.C.5   Are Rhode Island licensees required to obtain bonding or errors and omissions insurance?

E & O insurance, which protects licensees who are named in a lawsuit, is mandatory for all licensees in Rhode Island.

5.C.6 What is errors and omissions insurance?

E & O insurance is a type of coverage that protects brokers and affiliated licensees from loss due to errors, mistakes, and negligence. Rhode Island law requires all active licensees to carry E & O insurance. Licensees must annually submit evidence of compliance.

All licensees must file a certificate of insurance coverage with DBR with their initial applications and during each (two-year) license renewal cycle. The DBR will not renew a licensee without a certificate. DBR has the right to set the terms and conditions of the insurance policy. The minimum coverage was set at $100,000 for 2002. This, however, does not appear in any of the statutes or regulations. The standards adopted by the DBR include minimum liability limits, permissible deductible limits, and the permissible exceptions to the E & O insurance coverage. Licensees may not self-insure.

5.C.7 When must the errors and omissions insurance be activated?

A new licensee must provide proof of E & O insurance before licensure. Existing licensees must provide proof of E & O insurance when renewing their license.

6 Specialty Topics

Many other professions and issues touch real estate brokerage. This chapter discusses appraisal requirements, landlord tenant activities, and forms of ownership recognized in Rhode Island.

A. Related Real Estate Activities

6.A.1 What are Rhode Island state requirements for appraisers?

The Appraisal Division of the Department of Business Regulation licenses and regulates appraisers. DBR's Web site address is located at www.dbr.state.ri.us.

The Department of Business Regulation licenses "state certified real estate appraisers," those who perform real estate appraisals, with either a "general" certification or "residential" certification. A person (i.e., a real estate broker) may appraise residential property with four or fewer units for compensation by complying with applicable real estate regulations. Rule 26 defines what must be included in a broker price opinion. A real estate licensee need not be licensed as an appraiser to prepare a broker price opinion or Comparative Market Analysis (CMA).

The Real Estate Commission is currently (2002) considering a redefinition of the type of "appraisal" that a broker who is not licensed as an appraiser might perform.

6.A.2 Do home inspectors have to be licensed?

Yes and No. This is a true "Catch 22" situation. Effective July 1, 2001, Rhode Island law requires anyone who holds himself out to be a home inspector to be licensed or face statutory penalties. Two categories are named: associate home inspector and full-fledged home inspector.

However, the general assembly (state legislature), has not funded the law, so there is neither a Home Inspector Board nor staff to enforce it. Given state budget constraints, it is highly unlikely that this law will be implemented in the near future.

B.   Forms of Ownership

6.B.1 What forms of ownership are recognized in Rhode Island?

Rhode Island law recognizes the following basic forms of ownership of real property in addition to ownership by individuals, partners, corporations, limited liability corporations, etc.,: tenancy by the entirety (husband and wife with right of survivorship); joint tenancy (with right of survivorship); tenants in common (can convey an individual share of the property), and ownership in severalty.

6.B.2 Are dower and curtesy recognized in Rhode Island?

In Rhode Island, dower and curtesy have been abolished.

6.B.3 Can married couples designate separate and community property?

The Rhode Island Uniform Premarital Agreement Act allows prospective spouses to contract for future rights and obligations and to keep agreed property separate from community property.

C.   Other Forms of Ownership

6.C.1 What about partnerships, corporations, etc.?

Real estate brokerages in Rhode Island may include sole proprietorships, partnerships, limited operations, corporations, and subchapter S corporations.

6.C.2   What are time-shares? Do they have to be registered?

Time-shares are a form of ownership interest that includes the use of a property for a fixed or variable period of time. Time-share units that are sold by a developer must be registered with the Rhode Island Department of Business Regulation unless the developer offers them in increments of one at a time.

6.C.3   What laws cover time-share sales?

The Rhode Island Time-Share Act is divided into two parts. Sections 557A.4 – 557A.10 apply only to time-share programs located in Rhode Island, while Sections 557A.1, 557A.2, and 557A.11-20 apply to any time-share program, wherever located, that is marketed in Rhode Island.

6.C.4   Does a time-share salesperson require a real estate license?

No, the time-share salesperson is not required to first obtain a real estate license. Selling time-shares creates an "estate for years." Because this does not include the sale of real property, this does not constitute "real estate" for purposes of the real estate license law.

6.C.5   What disclosures must be provided?

Unless the sale qualifies for an exemption, a developer/seller/real estate licensee has a legal duty to provide the buyer with a public offering statement and any amendments to it. The statement is supposed to be made more than three days, excluding Sundays and holidays, prior to the buyer's execution of a purchase and sales agreement.

The public offering is prepared and provided by the original developer of the time-share project. In the case of a resale, the seller must provide a resale certificate that includes information such as time-share expenses, liabilities, liens, or court judgments against the property. The owner can obtain this information from the managing entity of the time-share.

6.C.6   Under what circumstances may a time-share purchaser rescind his or her contract?

There is a "cooling off" period. A buyer has the right to rescind a contract to purchase a time-share unit under certain circumstances.

The buyer can unilaterally terminate or void the agreement within three days, excluding Sundays and holidays, *after* the buyer receives the required information, or at the closing/transfer of title, whichever occurs first. Sometimes a buyer does not receive the required information until shortly before the closing or even at the closing, which means that the buyer could postpone or even terminate the closing.

If the buyer decides to terminate the agreement, the buyer must notify the seller by certified or registered mail or by hand delivery. The developer is legally required to return the deposit money to the buyer within 15 days after the developer receives the cancellation notice. If the seller fails to provide the buyer with the required materials at all, the buyer can claim as damages 10 percent of the sales price of the time-share unit in addition to other legal remedies.

6.C.7 What is the difference between a condominium and a cooperative?

Cooperatives and condominiums are examples of multiple owners of the same property. Articles of incorporation, bylaws, definitions, and restrictive covenants are all different and, therefore, due diligence is required before making a decision to purchase. The condo buyer receives a deed to real property. The coop buyer receives personal property in the form of a share of stock inseparable from the proprietary lease. The licensee who assists buyers in buying either type of property should always insist that the buyer read all relevant documents before entering into a purchase agreement.

6.C.8 What Rhode Island laws govern cooperatives and condominium ownership?

R.I.G.L. § 7-6.1 covers only housing cooperatives, which are geared towards "affordable" housing. There is no statewide guidance on these types of ownership.

6.C.9 How are unpaid association dues collected?

Note, all sums (association dues) assessed by the council of co-owners but unpaid for the share of the common expenses chargeable to any unit constitutes a lien and can be foreclosed on by suit from the council of co-owners or the association management company representing the co-owners. In other words, as a form of protest, nonpayment of association dues is not a good idea.

D. Landlord Tenant Issues

6.D.1 What Rhode Island law covers landlord tenant relations?

R.I.G.L. § 34-18 is titled Residential Landlord and Tenant Act. This chapter is designed to simplify, clarify, modernize and revise the laws governing the rental of dwelling units and the rights and obligations of both landlords and tenants and to encourage them to maintain and improve the quality of housing. In addition, the law insures that the right to the receipt of rent is inseparable from the duty to maintain the premises.

Anyone who manages even one unit should have a copy of this law and consult it frequently. The days have gone by when the landlord or manager could simply change the locks and toss the tenant's belongings into the street. Today, the tenant has enforceable rights, and if the landlord violates these rights, the landlord may be faced with financial penalties.

6.D.2 Do all leases have to be in writing?

In order to receive legal recognition in the judicial system, all lease agreements **over one year** must be in writing. Thus, an oral lease for less than a year is enforceable. However, it is important to remember: If it is in writing, you have a prayer; if it's oral, it's just air. It is best to get any lease in writing.

6.D.3 What specific procedures must a landlord follow to evict a tenant?

Eviction timetables are very precise, and a landlord must follow different procedures and deadlines depending on the purpose of the eviction: non-payment of rent; violation of the terms of the lease or tenancy agreement; termination of a week-to-week tenancy; or termination of a holdover tenant. Various mandatory notice and complaint forms can be found in the statute. Periodic tenancies such as month-to-month or even week-to-week agreements are more common than one year leases in Rhode Island.

6.D.4 What is the process for eviction for nonpayment of rent?

The landlord must send a written demand on a statutory form for the specific amount if the tenant's rent is 15 or more days in arrears. The required notice states that unless the tenant pays the rent in full within **5 days** of the notice, the lease/rental agreement is terminated, and the landlord will start eviction proceedings.

If the tenant does not make the full payment within the required five days, the landlord can start the eviction proceedings by filing a statutory "Complaint for Eviction for Nonpayment of Rent" and a statutory summons on the **6th day** from the mailing of the termination notice. When they file the complaint, landlords should definitely contact the clerk of the housing or district court to determine when the counting starts. If the tenant has not received a demand notice for unpaid rent in the previous six months, the tenant can pay the rent in full and court costs at the hearing. A hearing is held, if the case is not resolved sooner.

6.D.5   Is there a different eviction procedure for a breach other than unpaid rent?

If the tenant "materially" breaches the lease or other rental agreement, the landlord must send a statutory written demand notice warning the tenant that he or she must resolve the situation within **20 days.** If the tenant does not remedy the situation, the lease agreement terminates on the **21st day.**

For example, if a landlord wishes to stop a tenant from housing a pet or a roommate in violation of the lease, the tenant must remove the pet, guest, etc., prior to the termination date in order to avoid termination and subsequent eviction. Then, the landlord must file a "Complaint for Eviction for Reason Other Than Nonpayment of Rent" and a summons after the termination date specified in the demand notice.

6.D.6   How may a landlord terminate a periodic tenancy, i.e., week to week or month to month?

Either the landlord or tenant may terminate a week-to-week tenancy by providing a written statutory notice **10 days** in advance of the termination date. Prior to the expiration date, either landlord or tenant must give **30 days** notice for a month-to-month tenancy and **3 months** notice for a year-to-year tenancy.

6.D.7   What are the requirements for holding a security deposit (i.e., type of account, interest, limits on use, repayment, etc.)?

Rhode Island General Laws § 34-18-19 and 34-18-24 prohibit a landlord from collecting security deposits in excess of the value of one month's rent. Thus, upfront payments such as pet deposits or cleaning deposits are prohibited. The landlord is not required to pay the tenant any interest that may accrue on the deposit.

At the end of the tenancy, the landlord must return the security deposit within 20 days after the termination of the tenancy, or delivery of possession, or the tenant's providing the landlord with a forwarding address for the purpose of receiving the security deposit, whichever comes later. If the landlord wishes to retain any of the deposit, the landlord must send a letter or written notice to the tenant in which the landlord itemizes the damages.

At the end of the tenancy, the landlord may deduct unpaid rent and the cost of damage resulting from the tenant's failure to maintain the unit properly or failure to notify the landlord of problems with the unit. Damages may include dents and holes in the wall. Damages would not include ordinary wear and tear such as scuffed walls or chipped paint.

If the landlord does not comply with these requirements, the tenant can claim the amount owed to him plus double damages and attorney's fees.

6.D.8 Where does the landlord go to evict a tenant?

Municipal housing courts have original jurisdiction for eviction actions and related housing issues. However, because not all cities have housing courts, the landlord must first ascertain if there is one, and, if not, take the case to the appropriate district court.

At the present time, the state is divided into divisions, and each division has at least one district court. Licensees who manage property should start any legal process by determining the appropriate court.

6.D.9 Are there any other issues of which landlords should be aware?

As previously mentioned, the security deposit may not exceed one month's rent. However, there is mixed opinion as to whether Rhode Island law allows landlords to collect last month's rent in addition to a security deposit. The Landlord Tenant Act does not specifically discuss this issue. Tenants' attorneys argue that this is prohibited, while landlords' attorneys argue that absent a specific prohibition, landlords can collect the last month's rent. Licensees should consult with an attorney for guidance.

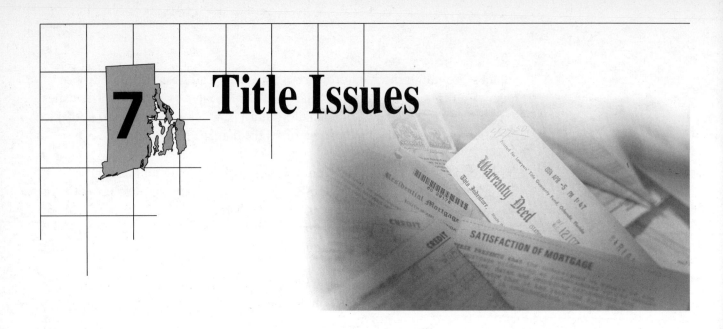

7 Title Issues

Encumbrances can affect the property value, its title marketability, and its transferability. This chapter covers basic information about Rhode Island specific rules regarding property taxes; encumbrances, such as licenses, easements, and adverse possession; and zoning regulations.

A.   Rhode Island Property Taxes

7.A.1   What is Rhode Island's fiscal year?

Rhode Island's fiscal year begins on July 1st of one calendar year and ends on June 30th in the next calendar year. Each town and city establishes its own fiscal year and sends its property tax notices at different times.

7.A.2   How are properties assessed?

According to statute, town "electors" vote to determine a tax based on assessments that are determined by the town assessors as of December 31st each year. Formal revaluation of properties is required to take place every ten years, which is one of the longest cycles in the country. During this long time period, properties can greatly shift in value by the time they are reassessed.

A number of municipalities revalued property at the peak of the real estate market in 2001, which led to large increases and furious taxpayers. As a result, the statute now requires municipalities to conduct a revaluation within nine (9) years of the date of the prior revaluation. Subject to state appropriation of funds, the municipality is supposed to conduct an update of real property every three (3) years from the date of the last revaluation.

7.A.3   Why do real estate agents need to know about property tax computations?

Agents should acquire basic knowledge about basic property tax assessments and time frames because property taxes can influence asking prices and offered prices. Tax assessors commonly use the selling price of recent sales to determine a property's value during the real estate tax revaluation process. Because most properties appreciate in value over time, the new owner should anticipate a property tax assessment increase after the upcoming real estate tax revaluation. As noted in 7.A.2, these increases can be substantial.

7.A.4   Can a property owner challenge a reassessment?

Yes, property owners or a tenant or tenants (who are required by their rental agreement to pay more than half of the real estate property taxes for the property in which they live) can file an appeal. They must use a statutory form and file with the local tax assessment office within 90 days from the date when the first payment is due.

The assessor has 45 days to review the appeal, render a decision, and to notify the taxpayer of the decision. Using a statutory form, the taxpayer may file an appeal challenging the decision of the tax assessor within 30 days after the decision is rendered. Taxpayers can also appeal within 135 days after they filed their appeals with the assessor to the local board of review if the assessor does not make a decision, or the fact that he has not rendered a decision. Ultimately, taxpayers can appeal to superior court if they remain unsatisfied.

7.A.5   How are tax rates determined?

Property taxes are used for the ordinary expenses and charges of the town, for the payment of interest and indebtedness, and for other purposes authorized by law. The rates are reflective of all approved state, city, schools, and special budgets. Tax rates also consider all sources of income. After deducting the anticipated ancillary revenue derived from governmental reimbursements, gasoline taxes, fines, sales taxes, motel/hotel taxes, etc., from the approved budgets, the remainder necessary to cover the costs of the approved budgets is divided by the appropriate taxable value to determine the tax rate.

Obviously, the tax levy varies with each taxing district. Decimal equivalent may be converted into a percentage. For example, a .035 tax rate would convert to 3.5 percent of the properties taxable value, which may then be converted to "mills," i.e., 35 mills.

7.A.6   Is there any possibility of reductions in taxes due?

Yes, some municipalities have created tax relief for certain property owners. Various towns have homestead exemptions for veterans, senior citizens, disabled people, etc. Property owners should always check with local authorities to ascertain if they are eligible for a reduction in property taxes. (Although these are referred to as "homestead" exemptions, they should not be confused with the state homestead exemption that is discussed in 7.A.7.)

7.A.7   What is Rhode Island's homestead exemption?

The state homestead exemption protects the homeowner from a forced sale of his or her principal residence by any unsecured lien holder. In Rhode Island, some of the homestead of every person is exempt from judicial sale where there is no statutory declaration to the contrary. The homestead exemption in Rhode Island is $150,000. Secured lien holders, such as lenders and owners who sell on contract, require the purchaser to waive their homestead rights as a prerequisite to the contract.

This exemption will not prevent the sale of the home in other situations. For a complete list of exceptions, one should consult R.I.G.L § 9-26-4.1. The debtor is not protected if the sale is forced for some of the following reasons:

- Nonpayment of taxes, sewer liens, water liens, lighting district assessments, and fire district assessments
- For a debt contracted prior to the acquisition of said estate of homestead
- For a debt contracted for the purchase of said home
- Upon an order issued by the family court to enforce its judgment for spousal support or the support of minor children
- Where a building or buildings are situated on land not owned by the owner of a homestead estate are attached, levied upon, or sold for the ground rent of the lot upon which the building or buildings are situated
- For a debt due to, or a lien in favor of, the department of human services and/or the state of Rhode Island for reimbursement of medical assistance, as provided for in § 40-8-15.

7.A.8   When are property taxes due?

Property tax statements are mailed out by each municipality, normally by the tax collector's office, at the start of the municipality's fiscal year. Rhode Island law requires municipalities to allow property owners to elect to pay their taxes in equal quarterly installments without interest or penalties instead of a lump sum. Some municipalities allow the payment of monthly installments.

7.A.9   How are the due taxes paid when the property is sold?

When the property owner sells, taxes are divided into **current taxes** (those due but not delinquent) and **prorated taxes** (those due but not payable). Rhode Island law provides that the selling taxpayer pays the taxes that are due but not delinquent and prorates those that are due, but not payable, to the buyer unless otherwise agreed by the parties.

7.A.10   What time frames must be followed?

The tax office sends out tax notices and due dates according to the fiscal tax year. Property owners should not assume knowledge of due dates if thcy move from one taxing authority to another. Each authority identifies due dates, and taxpayers need to be aware in order to avoid penalties. Each authority assesses its own penalties.

7.A.11   At what point are properties ordered sold at a tax sale?

A tax lien arises against a property once the tax assessment is made. If taxes remain unpaid, the tax collector can determine when to hold the tax sale provided that he or she gives at least three weeks notice prior to the time of sale to the owner, mortgagee, if any, and by public advertisement. Each town or county determines the appropriate sale date.

7.A.12   Does the delinquent taxpayer have any opportunity to "redeem" his or her property after a tax sale?

Yes, the former owner of the land, his or her heirs or assigns, can redeem the land prior to the filing of a petition for foreclosure by the town. The former owner can also redeem the property even if the town or another buyer has purchased the property for the back taxes.

If the town has purchased the land, thc prcvious owncr can redeem it by paying the town the amount for which the property sold plus a 10 percent penalty within six months after purchase. The owner can also pay an additional 1 percent of the purchase price for each month in addition to the six months. In other words, the former owner could redeem almost indefinitely as long as he is able to pay an additional 1 percent per month. Similar procedures apply if he or she redeems from a tax assignee from the town.

The former owner can redeem in much the same way from a buyer who has purchased the property from the town before the filing of a foreclosure petition or afterwards. The burden is on the new owner to file a petition of foreclosure in order to obtain a clear, clean title. In fact, the delinquent taxpayer can redeem the property from the person who paid the tax any time up until the new owner files a petition of foreclosure.

In this situation, the former owner must also reimburse the buyer the amount that was paid for the property, any additional taxes and costs incurred by the buyer, and a penalty of 10 percent of the purchase price if redeemed within six months after sale. If the redemption takes place after six months, the buyer must also pay 1 percent of the purchase price for each month in addition to the six months.

Complete information on tax sales and redemption may be found in § 44-9-19, 20, 21.

7.A.13   Is there anything else of which to be aware regarding property taxes?

Yes, there is. Rhode Island has a Real Estate Nonutilization Tax that is assessed against owners of vacant or abandoned property. This is a special assessment that is imposed by towns or cities to punish owners for failing to maintain or develop properties that have become eyesores or overgrown with weeds.

B.   Encumbrances

7.B.1   When do mechanics' liens apply? Who may claim them?

The Rhode Island Mechanic's Lien Act provides that a mechanic's lien is a statutory, equitable, lien created in favor of contractors, laborers, material-men, architects, and engineers who have performed work or furnished materials in the erection or repair of a building and who have not been paid. The subcontractors of architects and engineers may also file a mechanic's lien. The lien must be filed on the parcel of real estate where the material was used or the labor performed and must be filed in the county in which the real estate is located.

A "mechanic" who wishes to file a mechanic's lien must send the property owner a "Notice of Intention to Do Work" or a "Notice to Furnish Materials" or both. The forms include mandatory language and specific information, such as the amount owed, description of the work performed, etc., all of which must be included. The mechanic must file the Notice with the land evidence records in the municipality where the land is located within 120 days after completing the work.

However, if the property is in the process of being sold, the party seeking the lien must record the Notice within 40 days after completion of the work or furnishing materials in order to enforce it against a prospective, bona fide purchaser. This purchaser must be an arm's length buyer, not a relative or spouse.

7.B.2 Are there any other requirements for mechanics' liens?

Yes, the written contract between a licensed contractor and a property owner must state that the contractor, subcontractors, or materialmen may file a lien in accordance with the Rhode Island Mechanic's Lien Act.

7.B.3 How may easements be created in Rhode Island?

Easements in Rhode Island can be created by deed or by use. Easements can be created by mutual agreement, and maintenance easements can be used in homeowner association agreements.

A property owner may acquire a prescriptive easement by using someone else's property openly (visibly), notoriously, and without permission for a statutory period of ten years. Tacking is used to determine the time frame that has passed, and one owner is not required to have used the easement for the entire ten-year period.

7.B.4 What time frame must be observed for adverse possession (leading to ownership)?

In order to claim title to any ownership in real estate by adverse possession, a person must show that he or she has used the way, privilege, or other use openly, notoriously, and without permission for a period of at least ten years. Tacking is permitted.

To prevent adverse possession, the owner must serve written notice to anyone using in the land in question that the owner intends to dispute any right arising from such claim or use. If the owner has this notice served upon an authorized user of the property, he may record the notice in the recording office in the municipality in which the property is located.

7.B.5 Are there any other encumbrance issues of which to be aware?

Yes, however, they vary from town to town. Licensees should become familiar with requirements in each market area. Other issues include conservation restrictions to preserve open space and restrict development; affordable housing restrictions or covenants; private subdivision covenants or restrictions are all encumbrances that can greatly affect legal use of the property.

C.   Zoning Issues

7.C.1   *What is the source of zoning authority enjoyed by Rhode Island communities?*

The state of Rhode Island gives zoning and other land use authority to the local municipalities. Each local jurisdiction has the right to develop its own zoning regulations for the purpose of promoting the health, safety, morals, or the general welfare of the community, and the authority to regulate and restrict development.

7.C.2   *Under what conditions may a developer subdivide?*

Rhode Island law allows municipalities to charge impact fees after conducting needs assessments. The fees must be reasonably attributable to the impact of the development.

To ensure harmonious growth with community standards, land developers must conform to the municipality's subdivision and land development regulations. The regulations must be consistent with the municipality's comprehensive plan. The land must be surveyed and laid out so that the subdivision utilizes natural drainage and land contours. Often an environmental impact report is required with the application for subdivision approval. Plans have to be adopted by the municipality before they can be recorded.

After the subdivision plans are complete, plats are drawn of the land. The plat divides the land into lots. The plat is then submitted to the municipality for adoption. Often, the developer pays the costs for the streets and sewers, and then the streets and sewers are *dedicated* back to the municipality for its ownership and their future maintenance.

7.C.3   *Who or what regulates construction?*

Rhode Island is a home rule state which means that each local jurisdiction has its own land use regulations which are enforced by the local zoning authority, i.e., planning commission and boards of zoning appeals.

7.C.4   *Any special zoning terms?*

As mentioned previously, towns and cities have the ability to adopt cesspool and septic system inspection and replacement requirements that are stricter than those of the Department of Environmental Management.